WESTMAR COLLEGE LIBRARY
W9-BVR-348

Social Security:
A Reciprocity System Under Pressure

Other Titles in This Series

Also of Interest

Westview Special Studies in Contemporary Social Issues

Social Security: A Reciprocity System Under Pressure
Edward A. Wynne

Written in response to the controversies surrounding the funding of social security — controversies that are intensifying as the proportion of aged persons in our population increases — this book encourages a better understanding of the implicit reciprocal contracts that weld diverse age groups and people into a society. Focusing on the idea that the middle-aged group, or working generation, repays the old for help they received as dependent children, Dr. Wynne defines social security and other arrangements for the support of the elderly as reciprocity systems. He presents a cross-cultural survey of the nature and history of reciprocity systems, analyzes their common characteristics, and also explores the parallels between systems for aiding the aged and those for assisting other dependent groups — children, the infirm, the indigent.

Using the social security program as a vehicle for analysis, Dr. Wynne argues that current reciprocity systems are too depersonalized and bureaucratic. His conclusion is that people are giving and receiving more — typically through government structures — though enjoying it less, because the essential human elements of vital reciprocity systems have been undervalued. The main issue is not how much help is given, but rather the context in which it is delivered, and this is where our present system fails.

Dr. Wynne holds both LL.D. and Ed.D. degrees and is currently associate professor of education at the University of Illinois, Chicago Circle. He has served previously with the U.S. Office of Education at the Office of Economic Opportunity and has been an attorney for the National Labor Relations Board and associate general counsel to the Textile Workers Union of America.

Social Security:
A Reciprocity System Under Pressure

Edward A. Wynne

Westview Press / Boulder, Colorado

HD
7091
.W96

Westview Special Studies in Contemporary Social Issues

All rights reserved. No part of this publication may be reproduced or transmitted in any form or by any means, electronic or mechanical, including photocopy, recording, or any information storage and retrieval system, without permission in writing from the publisher.

Copyright © 1980 by Westview Press, Inc.

Published in 1980 in the United States of America by
  Westview Press, Inc.
  5500 Central Avenue
  Boulder, Colorado 80301
  Frederick A. Praeger, Publisher

Library of Congress Cataloging in Publication Data
Wynne, Edward.
  Social security, a reciprocity system under pressure.
  (Westview special studies in contemporary social issues)
  Includes bibliographical references and index.
  1. Social security. 2. Responsibility. I. Title.
HD7091.W96   368.4   80-18814
ISBN 0-89158-930-9

Composition for this book was provided by the author
Printed and bound in the United States of America

99206

CONTENTS

The things that people stand most in need of being reminded are, one would think, their duties; for their rights, whatever they may be, they are apt to attend to themselves....the great enemies of public peace are the selfish and dissocial passions...What has been the object , the perpetual and palpable object, of this declaration of pretended rights? To add as much force as possible to those passions, already but too strong, to burst the cords that hold them in; to say to the selfish passions — There, everywhere is your prey! to the angry passions, There, everywhere is your enemy!

—Jeremy Bentham[1]

INTRODUCTION

The word "perspective" is derived from the Latin "prospect." This root signifies that a more wholesome understanding of many phenomena is usually attained by acquiring some distance from their details. In pursuing such an overview, we are inevitably stimulated to learn about other activities or objects affecting our principal topic. Thus, when we climb a mountain to evaluate a parcel of land, we acquire knowledge about the property surrounding our focal point. After our climb and examination, we may even conclude that the plots surrounding our object of concern have more intrinsic significance than our initial focal point.

The declared aim of this book is to give readers an enriched understanding of the existing and foreseeable social pressures arising about the financing of the American social security system. But we cannot attain such an understanding without perspective. To acquire that perspective, we will have to step away from the operations of the system and even away from the situation in contemporary America. This stepping away will require an interdisciplinary effort.

Such a pursuit of perspective may generate some demands on readers — as does climbing a mountain. However, it may also stimulate valuable understandings. In any event, social security is our starting point.

Much of the energy of working-age adults is consumed in providing material and emotional help to members of younger or older age groups. And most of the help — the material resources and love — that sustains these dependents comes from this middle generation. The middle generation, almost by definition, always comprises the overwhelming voting majority of the society. Further, because of its productive responsibilities, it holds power by reason of its status as well as its numbers.

Some of the material resources supplied by the middle generation are provided through taxation, e.g., school taxes and social security deductions, but many of them are not measured by any structured accounting system. For assistance between age groups is comprised of more than giving help and affection to dependents or receiving it during our own dependency. All living Americans also enjoy many benefits derived from the sacrifices or "donations" of our now-dead predecessors: military heroes, dedicated researchers, political leaders, social reformers, explorers, and immigrant ancestors. And, in our own time, if America is to have a future, other now-living Americans must make equivalent sacrifices to provide our descendants with the material and social capital to meet the obscure but inevitable challenges that lie before our country.

The generalizations just propounded can lead us to consider a medley of statistics as well as social and psychological propositions relating to exchanges among age groups. For instance, in 1975, about 12% of America's Gross National Product was spent by agencies of the local, state, and federal government to provide formal education for the young and for social security assistance for the aged. Unquestionably, the many other forms of economic assistance concurrently provided to the young or the aged from other sources would raise the 12% figure to a much higher level. More significantly, beyond these modes of economic assistance, networks of families, relatives, and friends, inevitably make incalculable emotional sacrifices to assist dependent young and aged persons. Demographic forecasts reveal that the proportion of Americans classified as aged will increase over the next twenty to thirty years, and the proportion of the young will lessen. These changes ensure that the existing patterns of dependency among age groups will shift. Other relevant changes are also inevitable, as our definitions of dependency, and the needs and aspirations of dependent aged groups, evolve over time. These demographic and definitional shifts will affect the expenditure of over five trillion dollars over the next thirty years, and they will touch the day-to-day life of almost all Americans. We cannot take for granted that such vast changes will automatically occur in a coherent and appropriately incremental fashion: disjointed change, and the disorder that accompanies it, has been a frequent historical phenomenon.

The children and adults now involved in this elaborate web of transactions among age groups probably assume that the young now being helped while they are dependent will, when they mature, help their successors. They probably further assume that when they grow old they will again be assisted. In effect, a pattern of reciprocity is expected to be followed. At an extremely general level this assumption is "true." However, despite the vast sums of money involved in such exchanges, and the enormous emotional demands generated by the personal care of young and old dependents, there are almost no significant legal mechanisms that explicitly structure the nature of these exchanges. Nor are there significant formal mechanisms for the enforcement of reciprocal obligations among age groups. The truth is that the patterns of assistance among age groups are based only on implicit assumptions that, in themselves, presume the existence of a powerful amalgam of human trust. And practically speaking, no other arrangement is possible.

Thus, no contemporary middle-aged working adult is guaranteed any particular level of benefits from the social security system when he retires in the future, even though he paid into that fund while he was working. Nor is any parent planning to rear a child guaranteed that society will maintain an elaborate — or, indeed, even "adequate" — education system for that child. Future government payments from tax revenues to satisfy all such expectations are the product of a continuous political and social process. In the case of social security, the social security *fund* is not "funded": payments into the fund by current workers are used to support presently retired persons, and when persons who are now workers eventually retire, they presumably will receive their benefits from taxes paid by then active workers. But the level of taxes paid by workers who are active twenty or thirty years from now — when some of my readers retire — is determined by a political process which periodically amends the social security tax level. Obviously, that future tax level will reflect the wishes of a future voting majority composed principally of working-age persons. It is difficult to forecast how sympathetic future middle-aged workers will be to the pleas of the elderly, especially when those pleas must be evaluated against the needs of the workers' children or against their own natural desires for personal gratification.

Evidently, there is some form of fluid, continuing implicit reciprocal arrangement — a compact — among age groups in our society, as there must be in all societies. That compact shapes public and private actions about such obligations among age groups. The obligations may involve such matters as the maintenance of dependent age groups by the working population *en masse,* or the flow of help to individual young or old persons by their immediate relatives.

The compact apparently extends beyond exchanges among different living members of age groups. As already suggested, some of the most important contributions that benefit society are made by persons who may well not live long enough to receive the full emotional or material recompense they may "deserve": the soldier who dies to help his country, or the researcher, reformer, public leader, explorer, or immigrant whose sacrifices will largely benefit future generations. As we will see, these socially precious sacrifices on behalf of our posterity are motivated, at least in part, by conventions that encourage such dedicated persons to realize that their commitment will ultimately be recognized and rewarded by posthumous fame or memorialization. Such systems of social reciprocity are another form of compact among age groups. Only this form binds groups once living (and now dead), groups now living, and groups not yet born.

In a conceptual sense, reciprocal exchanges among age groups — despite their evident social and economic importance — are only a subset of all reciprocal exchanges among "dependent classes" and their larger society. Dependent classes include not only children and the aged, but the infirm, disabled, and inept, as well as persons otherwise unable to support themselves, either temporarily or permanently. I call help to such dependent groups "reciprocal" exchanges even though they may seem to be one-way donations. I do so deliberately. For dependent persons may shift to independence and in some way "repay" the donations. In other instances, where the apparent dependency is or may be permanent, the donors still expect certain "repayments," either from the recipients via deference or loyalty, or from other sources.

Almost all human societies, to some degree, have recognized a general obligation to dependent persons. The character of that obligation has varied widely, but the cross-cultural assumption has been that the unfortunate are to be pitied and assisted. Inevitably, there has been a strong relationship between any society's vision of its reciprocal exchanges with its dependents and its obligations to its young and old. Because of this relationship, changes in philosophies and policies affecting one group have spilled over to affect others. Thus, to have adequate perspective, any analysis of exchanges among age groups must simultaneously discuss the larger sphere of reciprocal exchanges among dependent classes and the producing society. As suggested earlier, such a discussion may both give us perspective on the social security situation and lead us to realize that some of the apparently "peripheral" matters raised are actually of greater import than we now comprehend.

The relationships we will consider are portrayed in the series of concentric circles in Figure I (see the following page). While social security reciprocity is presented as the core circle, I do not mean to imply that this reciprocity system is the essence of all reciprocity patterns. It simply means that, for the purposes of this book, I have chosen to use that system as my conceptual starting point.

Theoretically, the boundaries of the diagram (and its title) might be expanded to encompass all relationships in which people donate help, even though there is not apparent dependency, e.g., favors to business associates or to siblings. But I believe the aims of this book are best satisfied by remaining within the parameters described by the diagram.

To appreciate the significance of the categories of reciprocity defined by the diagram — and thus to see our present situation in perspective — I first examine the concept of reciprocity. This is followed by a discussion of the operation of the categories in other cultures. Next, I examine in particular the operation of reciprocity among the living and the dead. I then look at Western industrial society. And

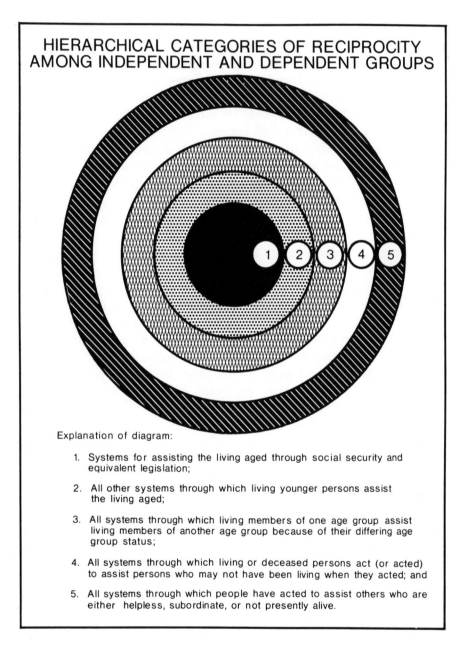

HIERARCHICAL CATEGORIES OF RECIPROCITY
AMONG INDEPENDENT AND DEPENDENT GROUPS

Explanation of diagram:

1. Systems for assisting the living aged through social security and equivalent legislation;

2. All other systems through which living younger persons assist the living aged;

3. All systems through which living members of one age group assist living members of another age group because of their differing age group status;

4. All systems through which living or deceased persons act (or acted) to assist persons who may not have been living when they acted; and

5. All systems through which people have acted to assist others who are either helpless, subordinate, or not presently alive.

Figure I

finally, I take the model derived from my earlier analyses and apply it to contemporary — or post-industrial — America. In that process, special emphasis is given to the category focusing on social security and equivalent legislation. The book concludes with a prescription and a forecast.

It is my hope that *Social Security* will provide readers with a fuller appreciation of our social security problems, as well as an understanding of the present and future tensions arising from donations to other dependent groups.

The parameters of the norm of reciprocity are comparatively indeterminate. In this respect, the norm is a kind of plastic filler, capable of being poured into the shifting crevices of social structures, and serving as a kind of all purpose moral cement.

—Alvin Gouldner[1]

CHAPTER 1

On Reciprocity

Reciprocity is a central characteristic of human society.[2] Reciprocity among independent and dependent groups — including age groups — is merely an instance of this characteristic. So let us first consider the general elements of the operation of reciprocity in society. Then, we can later examine the operation of those elements in exchanges among independent and dependent groups.

A reciprocity system is a set of conventions or values that stimulate persons or groups to donate goods or services to others with the expectation that the donors or their representatives will, in the future, receive similar consideration from the donees or their representatives. Such systems likewise stimulate, in the minds of the donees, an understanding that they incur obligations as a result of the donations they solicit or accept. Reciprocity systems can be broken down into different elements. Such a breakdown can facilitate analysis.

Among these elements are donors and donees (and their representatives); and either or both of these categories can be groups or individuals. The subject matter of the donation can be either tangible or intangible. Each act of delivering a donation and each subsequent return of a counterdonation, constitutes a transaction, while the complete sequence of donation and counterdonation constitutes an exchange, or what may sometimes be called a reciprocal exchange. Transactions and exchanges may be either immediate — and occur in a limited period of time and/or a restricted space — or remote. Exchanges can be either discrete — with participants clearly identifiable as donors and donees, or continuous with such an elaborate variety of transactions as to make it impossible to classify or bound the steps of the process. The obligation created by the donation may be either direct — the donee must "repay" the donor — or indirect — the donee must "repay" some representative of the donee in exchange for the original donation. The means for the enforcement of reciprocity after a donation has passed can be either formal (codified, explicitly accepted and tied to some public enforcement structure) or informal (unwritten, tacitly accepted and enforced by informal rewards and sanctions). The goods and services involved can include not only material objects, but also physical help and advice and possibly acts or words symbolizing gratitude and deference; the qualifier "possibly" is necessary because signs of deference represent commitments which may only later be translated into "firm" counterdonations. The complexities of the operation of reciprocity systems become clear when we consider the contrast between exchanges involving:

(a) An individual donor and donee, who have a tangible, immediate, discrete, direct exchange subject to a formal enforcement or,

(b) A group that directs a representative to donate intangible goods through a remote transaction to a donee group who will indirectly repay with intangible, remote, continuous counterdonations to a yet to be created group that will be representative of the donee, and where this whole procedure is subject only to informal enforcement. (When General Pershing led the first American troops ashore in France during World War I, he said, "Lafayette, we are here." That statement portrays the landing as a tangible, remote, indirect, counterdonation, enforced through informal means. Incidentally, it ennobles the conduct of both the French and American peoples.)

In industrial society — and to a lesser degree, in pre-industrial societies — legal systems are an important means for formally structuring reciprocal exchanges between private parties and groups.[3] The civil law essentially defines the nature of such obligations and provides the means of enforcement. But even in industrial society, the variety of human needs, and the necessity of flexible networks for collective action, have placed many reciprocity systems outside the legal system.[4] And, in pre-industrial societies, the forms of such non-legal obligations are even more elaborate.

Learning About Reciprocity

Obviously, a variety of reciprocity systems will exist in any society, and even more diversity will exist among societies. As a result, forms of reciprocity are often culture-bound. Furthermore, such forms are restrained in particular cultures by the effects of social class conventions; in other words, the exchanges that members of a class or group transact with one another are subject to different conventions than are interclass exchanges or exchanges within other classes. These factors mean that particular symbols, circumstances, questions of status, and elements of timing will be involved in deciding whether any particular individual act should be perceived as part of an exchange. Due to these variables, a person's ability to participate in a reciprocal activity — either through individual action, or as a member of a group — *is learned*. Technically speaking, we would say that members of a society or class are socialized to its systems of reciprocity. Such socialization is necessary because no person "naturally" knows: whether a particular common gesture is a compliment or an insult; what obligations — if any — are presumably created by the acceptance of certain "gifts"; what acts or donations, on what occasions, are appropriate for engendering certain obligations in others; and what are the probable consequences of failing to meet some reciprocal obligation.

But socialization to reciprocity is more than a matter of comprehending a set of explicit and implicit symbols and practices. While the forms of reciprocity need to be learned, it is also probable that without persistent social support, individual citizens will refuse to accept or apply the very concept of reciprocity.[5] One could argue that infants apparently intuitively apply reciprocal concepts in their contacts with others; even at very young ages, infants typically smile back when adults smile at them, and sometimes infants smile to provoke smiles in adults. Such exchanges do suggest some basic predisposition to reciprocal conduct. However, it is also true that these predispositions are usually vigorously reinforced by the caretakers of children. We let the infant know that we are pleased with his reciprocation. Further, when children do not easily share with others, they are often criticized by their care-takers. Indeed, any observer of children's conduct can note innumerable instances of "naturally" selfish or non-reciprocal acts. Oftentimes, these instances of egocentricity are described as "childish" conduct: they are sometimes tolerated for awhile, but the expectation is that they will be abandoned as the child develops greater capability for perception and is exposed to more learning experiences.

This predisposition of infants and children to engage in reciprocity is constrained by (a) their developmental level — some concepts relating to exchanges are beyond their grasp, and (b) their innate human selfishness — which is just as "natural" as their reciprocal instincts.[6] Children's conflicting dispositions about reciprocity and selfishness are gradually tempered because a child lives and grows must be maintained by other human beings. By reason of living in such an environment, the young child routinely finds himself in situations where reciprocal conduct is the norm. Thus, role models are put before the child, and his care-takers (typically) increasingly demand that he accept the conventions of reciprocity appropriate to the environment (and consonant with his developmental level). The process partially sublimates the child's egocentric drives into acceptable reciprocal transactions.

An optimistic observer of this whole process would say that the child is born into a family, displays certain tendencies towards reciprocity, and refines those tendencies as it matures. A more cynical — or sophisticated — observer might say that the child displays both egocentric and reciprocal tendencies, and that the process of social living socializes the child to subordinate some of its egocentric drives into reciprocal conduct. In other words, socialization to reciprocity is no more "natural" than learning how to drive a car, or to read or speak English.[7] After we have learned how to engage in these actions, we carry them out without conscious thought; however, without appropriate learning structures, we would not know how to do them. It may be that some persons have greater innate talents for some of these activities than do other persons — and, similarly, some persons may have greater innate capability for learning about reciprocity — but, without learning situations, there would be no drivers, readers, or English-speaking people. And, with better learning situations, almost everyone in American society — regardless of his handicaps — can attain a minimum level of these skills.

The model of socialization to reciprocity just sketched is enormously simplified. Thus, it only considers exchanges between individuals. But many important reciprocal transactions are between groups: exchanges involving corporations, or tribes, or nations, or voting blocs. These exchanges are only feasible if many of the members of each entity party to the exchange share some conventions with each other. Thus, when America and the Soviet Union consider whether to sign a joint treaty for arms limitation — that is, when they decide whether to engage in a particular exchange — the viability of their proposed treaty depends upon a variety of factors related to reciprocity.[8] Do the members of each society have a common understanding among themselves about what their collective obligations will be, and does each society, and many of its members, have an appropriate understanding of what the other sees its obligations to be? And so on.

Evidently, continuous intergroup reciprocal transactions require that the numerous individuals, upon whom the maintenance of the exchange ultimately depends, have a comparatively sophisticated understanding of the elements of a complex process. We can see that learning the forms of reciprocity appropriate to different situations is a lifelong challenge, since the diversity of interpersonal and intergroup exchanges that can arise is infinite. The infant, child, or adolescent learns the reciprocal conventions related to his constrained status and developmental level, and, as he matures, learns more elaborate and demanding conventions as he ages. A society that does not socialize its young to such elaborate conventions will gradually disintegrate into progressively smaller groups where less complex conventions can still persist, and where exchanges can occur; and if no children at all were socialized to reciprocity, systems for the maintentance of reciprocity could not persist, and human life would shortly expire. (Indeed, one interpretation for the phrase "No one here understands me," is that the "me" involved has not been socialized to engage in reciprocity in the prevailing environment. And, without exchanges, one is inevitably alone.) Conversely, if a society wishes to socialize maturing children to participate in increasingly larger-scale transactions, it strives to encourage them to support steadily larger reciprocal systems. But how are the young socialized to accept and apply such increasingly complicated information, and how does the society overcome the powerful human potential for selfishness, which evidently coexists with the tendency to engage in reciprocal conduct?

How We Are Socialized to Reciprocity

Our simplified model of socialization to reciprocity can help us to analyze the typical events and structures that help societies rear adults committed to participating in reciprocal relationships. As already suggested, this process of socialization starts simply and slowly becomes more complex. A parent reinforces the infant's tendency to structure some of his conduct to as to please others: he smiles back when the infant smiles and looks at his face. Gradually the child is introduced into situations where he is simultaneously relating to both parents in their presence. He must then learn how to govern his conduct in the light of each parent's relation to himself and their concurrent transactions with each other. Later, the child can be reinforced to engage in tangible donations, e.g., helping clean up, or making small presents, which may lead to parental counterdonations. The parents also periodically make tangible, clearly labeled donations to the child and suggest that reciprocity "requires" the child to make appropriate responses — either "Thank you," or later counterdonations to the donor. Clearly, the model we are considering puts considerable emphasis on direct, tangible and intangible, immediate transactions that are enforced through informal structures. Many of these transactions are continuous — part of a stream of exchanges — rather than discrete.

Up to this point, the discussion of parent/child exchange has implied the existence of a "balanced" reciprocal relationship between the two parties. This portrayal is only partially accurate. There is also a vast discrete exchange occurring between the parties. This exchange involves the largest proportion of the "valuables" that parents typically donate to their children: their time, emotional energy, and often a great many material resources. These enormous donations are direct, both tangible and intangible, and essentially part of a remote, discrete exchange. Thus, while the child may perceive the simple, day-to-day sacrifices a parent makes on his behalf, he is incapable of appreciating the large, pervasive constraints that parents bear as a result of the responsiblities of parenthood. Those constraints, which are really donations, are so inherent in the status of parenthood as to be incomprehensible to the child.

However, the parents, as adults, are typically socialized to translate transactions into exchanges. This normal parental perspective is reflected in two strategies. One strategy is for parents to aim to socialize the child to expect to provide help (or counterdonations) for his parents in their old age, in exchange for the enormous donations he received from them during his dependency. This strategy explicitly recognizes the remote, discrete nature of the bulk of parent-to-child donations. A second, and concurrent, strategy of parents is to symbolically transform their one-direction donations into an immediate continuous exchange, by expecting the child to reciprocally "donate" love, respect, and obedience back to them. In other words, "Honor thy father and mother." This largely intangible, continuous, direct exchange transforms the parents' acts of commitment and sacrifice into a symbolically immediate exchange. This exchange serves a number of ends: it satisfies the parents' emotional need for donations in exchange for donations; it simplifies the demands made on parents by socializing their children to day-to-day responsiblity and obedience; and it immediately symbolizes the child's remote, discrete obligation to repay the parents' present donation later with equivalent tangible and and intangible resources.

Power, Motives, and Socialization

It may seem that the "motives" just attributed to parents for socializing their child to obedience — and respect — are largely selfish. In other words, the socialization process is run for the benefit of the parents rather than that of the child. However, this is an oversimplified statement. Without some modicum of obedience, respect, and trust from the child, the parents' task would become unmanageable, to the detriment of both the child and the parent. Furthermore, the parents, when they made their decision to become parents, had before them some vision of the relationship that would exist between them and their child. Presumably, they expected that relationship would be reciprocal — not one-way. But many of the parents' donations are intangible and remote; and a child cannot be essentially a donee for perhaps twenty years, and then suddenly be expected to reciprocate. And so parents are constrained to devise and encourage symbolic counterdonations signifying honor and respect — intangible dodations — that can permit the child to immediately participate in exchanges. The child also is being reared to live in an essentially reciprocal adult world; he cannot hope to survive acting solely as either donor or donee. Thus, unless the parents socialize the child to symbolically respond to their own enormous donations, the child may fail to appreciate the complex reciprocal nature of adult life and become enmeshed in a narcissistic cocoon. Such isolation would be self-destructive and other-destructive. Finally, we must recognize that even children, in many families and cultures, are expected to contribute tangibly and immediately from very young ages. The levels of such contributions are affected by many variables; however, in some cultures, six year olds are important family helpers, while in others, "children" are solely donees until they are sixteen or eighteen. Inevitably, a child's early involvement in such activities simplifies his learning about reciprocity.

We have just considered a model, or simplified abstraction of the parent/child socializing process. The nature of that model implies that parents must exercise considerable ingenuity and authority throughout this process. Ingenuity and authority are needed because there are many barriers to effective socialization to reciprocity. On the one hand, the child's innately selfish drives must be contained. On the other hand, a decent degree of individual self-regard is essential to effective adulthood — so a person can have the determination to protect himself from the occasional selfishness and ignorance of others — and thus the containment of selfishness must leave some room for healthy self-defense. Again, children and their parents are all going to have differences in innate temperament and cognitive ability, and appropriate adaptations to these differences must be devised. Finally, the material resources of families and the external environment around families will differ, and this can affect the operation of the socialization process.

Despite these challenges, there are resources available to parents to assist them in the process. The simpler forms of a child's selfishness and narcissism gradually become so burdensome to most parents that they are compelled to learn how to diminish them. That learning may be a process of trial and error, but it must be pursued if only in self-defense. (As we can imagine, the teaching of self-respect is a more complex matter: parental faulture in this particular can be concealed for longer periods of time.) Children's psychological and cognitive capabilities for engaging in more complex acts of reciprocity also gradually increase: this is not to say that they will "naturally" engage in such exchanges, but to emphasize that as they grow older, they are capable of learning more. In addition, societies typically grant a great deal of authority to parents and do not restrict it with complex judicial structures. Such authority provides parents with the power and flexibility they may need to deal with subtle reciprocity issues. For instance, a parent may choose to reprimand "sassiness," or hostile glances (which are inconsistent with deference and obligation) even though no court could judge what acts constitute such conduct.

Parental power is reinforced by the child's inevitable ignorance and helplessness. The child perceives that he should obey his parents because they know about dangers and opportunities he cannot yet recognize. The social structure in many societies also surrounds parents with supporting persons and experiences: older relatives who can offer child-rearing advice based on first-hand experience; other families whose easily apparent successful and unsuccessful child-rearing patterns can offer role models; systems of human relations that give adolescents, who are parents-to-be, experience in helping adults in child-care; and bodies of collective wisdom about how to "parent," ranging from proverbial knowledge to how-to-do-it courses and books. Still, for most parents throughout history, perhaps the most significant factor that has assisted them in socializing their own children to reciprocity has been an intense drive to succeed in that process, *since the parents' own lives depend on it.*

The fact is that the child inevitably uses the resources of the family. Unless the family is comparatively affluent, it is compelled — in order to survive — to socialize the child to strive to begin to reciprocate as soon as possible. Indeed, in many families and cultures, the process of such socialization is essentially non-theoretical: the chickens must be fed and the dishes washed; and so, without a lot of analysis, the parents say, "Do it or else ...." Furthermore, the parents — if they live to an old age — will eventually become non-producers and must often rely on the "loyalty" of their adult children to help support them during this period. The desperate need to succeed predisposes parents: to pursue knowledge about how to socialize children; to carefully examine the implications of their own and their children's conduct in the light of reciprocal principles; and to focus their parent/child relations on the cultivation of reciprocity. In effect, the need to socialize children to reciprocity provides parents with a very clear intellectual framework for managing parent/child relations.

On Attributing Intent

I have used the pattern of attributing conscious intent to many aspects of parent/child relations, even though such consciousness frequently does not exist. Essentially many patterns of parental conduct have been unconsciously learned, or they are the product of conscious learning situations that have been forgotten. To consider an analogy about learning in another area, most of us have forgotten how we deliberately learned to read, and we now regard reading as a "natural" act. But it is only natural because the learning occurred so long ago that we forget the circumstances, frustration, and tensions that probably surrounded it. Similarly, for most parents, learning about parenting occurred through such an incremental and pervasive process that they now do not remember the steps involved.

In order to anaylize or improve parent/child reciprocal relations, we must clarify and scrutinze this comparatively ignored learning process, just as someone concerned with improving the teaching of reading must engage in equivalent dissection of how people learn to read. In the case of reading, the dissection would show that beginning readers start to learn by deliberately doing things that they later perform unconsciously. Thus, the attribution of conscious intent to much parent conduct is not a misleading fiction; such intent was conscious for many parents during the state they "learned" such conduct. Their current conduct — which may consist largely of intuitive responses — is only "intuitive" because of their earlier deliberate decisions to act in such-and-such a way.

There may be some parents who act purely on "rote," who follow or apply patterns of conduct they learned without ever appreciating or having comprehended their rationale — like persons who have learned to drive an auto without understanding the principles of internal combustion engines. But even these rote parents are applying principles which were learned because they are generally approved. However, in order for these principles — which foster effective parent/child reciprocity — to have won general approval, some class of persons, at some time, probably recognized a relationship between such principles and the efficient operation of families in society. Therefore, even if some parents never weighed their motives for following particular patterns of socialization — except to realize "It's what everybody does" —we can properly attribute a rationale to a society with such patterns. And the parents can be considered instruments of that rationale.

In sum, in a number of families, parents have a series of conscious motives for socializing their children to reciprocity, which motives are congruent with the preceding analysis. Even when those motives are absent in a particular family, they still pervade the society — which is a macrocosm of the family — and the family tends to act in ways congruent with social norms.[9] Thus, the attribution of specific motives to parental conduct vis-a-vis children is justified. As we will see, such attribution is a powerful tool for analysis — for, if the circumstances fostering such motives have changed, we can ultimately look for changes in parental conduct and the kind of children and adults that are reared. We will return to this point later.)

Society as a Socializing System

The two-parent/child family model we have been considering is apparently a simple reciprocity system. Despite its simplicity it contains, in its workings, many of the facts found in complex reciprocity systems. Thus, it is really a combination of simplicity and complexity. It is simple because the number of persons involved is limited, they share many important common values, and the distribution of informal enforcement authority during most of the child's minority is comparatively clear. It is complex because, though many of the exchanges involved are tangible, immediate, discrete, and direct, they steadily become more intangible, remote, continuous, and indirect. As a result, the increasing complexity of in-family reciprocity provides a good simulation of the reciprocity problems the child will face in later life.[10] Incidentally, even the "simpler" aspects of in-family reciprocity can be complicated by other factors: the child may have siblings or his nuclear family may be integrated into a functioning extended family, where the child will speedily begin to have significant reciprocal relationships with various relatives.

Despite the critical role of the nuclear family in socializing a child to reciprocity, the knowledge transmitted through the family is only the foundation of a prolonged learning process. The child and adolescent, as he grows toward adulthood, receives donations from an enlarging group of donors, and is expected to provide counterdonations in increasingly complex reciprocal exchanges. As a result, he is gradually exposed to more elaborate learning about reciprocity. Perhaps the peak of this learning process is reached at the attainment of adulthood, where the former child is launched from the family into the comparatively impersonal world. But even after this demanding transition, the adult will still be faced with challenges of learning more about reciprocity throughout his life.

Before we consider a general model of out-of-family learning about reciprocity, it is appropriate to identify some of the "motives" which provoke societies — acting as representatives of their collective citizens — to devise and maintain such models. And, once again, as in the case of the family, it is evident that attributed motives — even though they are only held consciously by a limited number of citizens — can still be important tools for comprehending this social process. Societies "want" children to grow into adults who are socialized to practice reciprocity because adults who do not effectively practice reciprocity are destructive to others.

One of the most important things in the world to each person is the attitudes and conduct of other persons. Other adults have the potential, if they dare, to try to be simply donees, or takers, rather than participants in exchanges. Thus, they can rob us. Or they can become alcoholics or drug addicts, and expect us to assist them by our payment of taxes for welfare, medical care, and rehabilitation institutions. They can simply be incompetent or barely productive, and unable to help defend or advance society, or they may raise children who will commit crimes or otherwise burden us. We might liken

This topic of mediating agencies requires amplification. Mediating agencies are institutions or widely accepted symbols (maintained by such institutions) which assist the maintenance of reciprocal patterns. Such agencies are important in the management of intangible, remote, and indirect transactions. They grow in significance as the subject matter of transactions becomes more abstract, as transactions persist over long periods of time or extend over large geographic areas, and as counterdonations are due from persons who were not party to the original donation. Finally, as the subject matter of exchanges becomes more valuable — regardless of their nature — more powerful enforcement structures, relying on mediating agencies, become increasingly necessary. Obviously, mediating agencies can assume many forms: monetary systems; institutions — such as the Catholic Church or the U.S. Marines — which maintain conventions that solemnize commitments; lending agencies and stock markets; political structures that facilitate transactions between voting blocs; and a great variety of agencies that collect and distribute funds or resources as part of transactions or exchanges.

If mediating agencies are to sustain remote exchanges, they must persist (have an "institutional memory") and exercise influence over a wide geographic area. Because of this need for persistence and size, the agencies become institutions and develop a life of their own. This life often assumes greater importance than the agency's relationship with any individual person or exchange. Such "impersonality" is part of the agency's social value: it renders the agency's role predictable and reassures persons who rely on it to enforce exchanges. (Incidentally, the agency, in order to meet the inevitable costs of its operations, will typically levy some form of charge or tax on its users or members.) In any event, the growing child has to learn about the role of mediating agencies in exchanges. Without such knowledge, he will be restricted to only the simplest exchanges or to "exploitation" by persons who use such agencies to their peculiar advantage. Much of this learning will occur outside of the family. Of course, the agency, too, often wants children socialized to use the agency in transactions and exchanges: such usage increases the size and prestige of the agency. However, the goals of individual agencies are not always congruent with the best interests of individual users: furthermore, individual citizens and competing mediating agencies may (to advance their own self-interests) mislead the recruit as to the nature of certain agencies. And so we have a complex learning problem. We must finally recognize that "society," itself is the ultimate mediating agency. It is a conglomeration of individuals and varied mediating agencies that theoretically exists in order to facilitate an innumerable variety of transactions. And, like the lower level mediating agencies we have just been characterizing, society, too, necessarily assumes a life of its own, beyond the significance of the individual exchanges among its citizens and groups. But, in the end, the test of a society's viability is its ability to foster an appropriate mix of discrete and continuous, reciprocal exchanges among its citizens, and between its citizens and other societies.

Society as a Socializer

Normally, the child does gradually leave the socializing patterns of the family, and become subject to those "maintained" by the larger society.[13] The nature of this leavetaking varies among cultures. Sometimes, it is symbolized by a dramatic rite-of-passage. But even when there is such a dramatization, the leavetaking inevitably contains substantial elements of incrementality. Before it occurs, the child is in some ways actings as an adult, and after it occurs, the adult is still subject to many of the actual (if not symbolic) characteristics of childhood. This is not to imply that puberty rituals are meaningless, but simply to suggest that no matter how a society structures moments of passage, it still must arrange for teaching to occur before and after such moments.

When and how does this teaching by society occur? To put it baldly, societies — as extra-family agencies — begin socializing infants to reciprocity from the moment they are born, and continue to do so until they die. Perhaps the process can be characterized by a bell shaped curve. Thus, the curve of in-family socialization peaks sometime in late childhood, and begins gradual decline. The role of society as the principal socializer enlarges as the curve of in-family learning declines. However, the child and society are at all times engaged. Society's role begins with the ceremonies that typically surround birth. These activities are not apparent to the infant. Still they involve the parents, the immediate family, and friends. Through such ceremonies, these adults, and the infant's siblings, are informed of the anticipated relationship between the infant and the society. They are directed to treat the growing infant as if he were participating in a conscious reciprocal relationship with the society, and to "instruct" him in how to carry out that relationship. (Godparents are an example of adults who are explicitly assigned such roles.) Society first asserts its authority by reminding those about the infant of what instructions they are to proffer. From this moment on, society continues to intensify participation. The infant, and later the child, sees society personified in the symbols, poetry, and folklore that penetrate the household. Outside the home, the architecture, statues, parades, ceremonies, flags, and banners communicate images of benevolent but demanding authority.[14] These varied devices demonstrate to the child the donations society has provided and will provide on his behalf. They also present to the child models of older persons actively engaging in making counterdonations to the society or its components. The devices suggest to the child that he, too, someday will be expected to make similar counterdonations. Indeed, the child will even come to associate the idea of being able to make such counterdonations with the attainment of adult power.

The child will also gradually come in contact with the activities of various public and private institutions, especially mediating agencies: churches, markets, systems of production, schools. These entities will symbolically stress their relationship to the implicit reciprocity systems that bind and maintain society. Such symbolic articulation can, of course, also reinforce the earlier socialization of the adult members of an institution; however, the articulation can be even more important as a learning device for potential or new "members." Thus, many adults who, themselves, are already "fully" socialized to reciprocity, will be expected to continue to communicate symbolically their commitment — so that less socialized persons may be instructed. The society that gradually unfolds before the child will be perceived as demanding. However, the child is simultaneously being reassured that those demands can be met, and that the overall effect of this edifice is beneficent and protective. After all, there are demands made on the child by the family, and the child recognizes that, by satisfying those demands, he can increase his own control of his environment. Evidently, the child concludes that a similar pattern pervades adult society:

individual citizens and groups give and receive a variety of donations, and through such reciprocal exchanges, social life is maintained and enriched.

A crucial problem in the process of socialization to reciprocity occurs when the child or adult begins to perceive the conflicts that may arise between his primary group loyalties — to his family, community, or ethnic group — and those to the larger society. Both of these mediating entities — the primary group and the larger society — have participated in his socialization. Often, each of the entities have a need for the continuing cooperation of the other. The inferior entity (i.e., the primary group) needs the superior entity in handling large-scale challenges or opportunities. The superior entity needs the inferior one because children and adults cannot persistently maintain satisfactory identifications (i.e., develop loyalties) to remote, large, and necessarily impersonal institutions. Thus, the survival of the superior entity is partly dependent upon the persistence of vital inferior entities that enlist citizens and simultaneously remind them of their relationships to both inferior and superior entities. However, it is predictable that some of the exchanges between these inferior and superior entities will involve intangible, remote (and often indirect) exchanges, enforced through informal procedures. Such exchanges are often fraught with ambiguity. This ambiguity will inevitably lead to sporadic conflicts over what obligations have been created, and how powerful they are. On such occasions, individual citizens who simultaneously belong to two overlapping entities will be subject to growing stress centered about the question: whose cause will they favor? The prevention and management of such interinstitutional and intrapersonal stress are critical elements of social policy.

When such conflicts arise, the superior entity (and its managers) may be tempted to override the interests of the inferior entity in an effort to simplify the problems of system maintenance. Similarly, within the inferior entity, there may be a temptation to secede from the superior entity (if this is possible) so as to maintain the integrity of the inferior unit. Sometimes, such strategies are warranted. But more often, some measure of compromise is appropriate. The feasibility of such compromise is determined by the flexibility of the members of the superior and inferior entities, and the imagination of their leaders. The quality of this flexibility is highly dependent upon the nature of socialization to reciprocity to which the citizens have been subject. In other words, adults in the conflicting systems will perceive that they owe "loyalties" — as a result of benefits received — to one or the other, or both, of these entities. To the extent that these loyalties are adequately diversified, individual citizens will strive to bring about a compromise and the maintenance of both entities. But without such diversification, destructive conflict will result. In any event, a superior entity must strive to implant a sense of loyalty in its future citizens — simultaneously, however, it must endeavor not to eliminate the vital subordinate entities which will form the core of its citizens' day-to-day lives.

Of course, most of the exchanges that affect adult citizens in their daily lives do not directly involve formal public and private entities; they usually occur among family members, friends, neighbors, or co-workers. Still, there is an important relationship between these "mundane" exchanges — which might be called micro-exchanges — and those between citizens and major institutions. Both micro- and macro-exchanges involve many of the same conceptual elements. They place mutually supporting models of conduct before many children and adult citizens. The child may liken reciprocal relations in the family to those prevailing between his family and the state; in addition, he may fantasize his future relationships with employers in terms of his vision of family/state relations. Obviously, these projections are ridden with distortion and misunderstandings. Despite these shortcomings, the vision of beneficent reciprocity I have attributed to the child contains an essentially accurate perception of society. Any effective and continuing society must be based on a network of public and private actions that are routinely converted into continuous or discrete exchanges: when we smile, people smile back; when we work for pay, we are paid; when loyal and responsible citizens get in trouble, the state will protect them; and so on. Of course, these general principles have many exceptions, and persons who make donations must still evaluate their means of enforcing the reciprocal obligations they have created, i.e., will they be repaid? Nonetheless, the observance of reciprocal patterns is the basic norm. Without such observance, social life would dissolve. And so the child's perception is essentially "correct." One task of any socialization system is to help the child refine that initial perception, to make it, perhaps, a bit more guarded and sophisticated. But it never intends to help him forget the central truth. After all, even adults whose prattle is burdened with pervasive cynicism run their day-to-day lives as if they expected to be paid for their work and receive essential value for what they pay. Any person who believed that even 25% of his donations was not reciprocated would feel deep distress.

Independent Donors, Dependent Donees

Now that we appreciate the general principles of socialization to reciprocity, let us turn to the particular principles that govern exchanges among dependent and independent groups, as portrayed in the diagram in the Introduction. By "dependents," I mean persons who are (a) alive, dead, or unborn at the time of the donation, or (b) otherwise unable to proffer counterdonations of the same apparent value as the donation at the time of its giving. The phrase "same apparent value" does not preclude the dependent donees from offering the independent donor symbolic counterdonations, such as gratitude or deference; and such acts may signify the creation of an obligation repayable in the future; however, symbolic donations, while not valueless, are obviously of a more complex nature than immediate repayments.

Members of all societies make donations to many dependent groups. Still, some general principles governing such activities can be summarized. All members of any society spend significant proportions of their lives in the status of dependent donees: they will be helpless children; transitorily ill or injured; temporarily unable to earn a livelihood because of situations beyond their control (e.g., an economic depression or a drought); or decrepit and aged. Unless a society evolves a means of generally handling such inevitable dependencies, it will become extinct. Another reason societies must help many dependents is that persons currently independent will perceive that, if they become dependent (as is highly likely) in an "uncaring" society, they will be left bereft. Given this powerful threat, currently independent people in an uncaring society will either emigrate to a more humane society, or vigorously strive to change the existing policies. In other words, human beings will make only a modest or transitory investment in an environment which will refuse to help them in time of future distress.

The preceding abstract discussion will gain more focus if we illustrate it with an instance from pre-Christian (but Western) history. Under Mosaic law, a Jewish male was obligated to marry the widow (who was a dependent donee) of his deceased immediately elder brother.[15] The utilitarian elements of this requirement were plain. The widow was provided with a form of insurance. The parties to a proposed marriage were given an incentive to loyalty and commitment: the groom with male siblings could offer his proposed bride some assurance of support in the event of his premature death. Of course, all male siblings (and their brides) in a family shared this benefit: each brother was a co-guarantor of the next one. And the "guarantee" was reinforced via powerful mediating systems: the Mosaic law and the entire fabric of Jewish community life. In particular, the law provided that if a brother failed to meet this obligation of a sibling's widow (and that brother was a potential independent donor), the widow "shall come unto him in the presence of the elders, and loose his shoe from off his foot, and spit in his face, and *shall* answer and say 'So shall it be done unto that man that will not build up his brother's house' (italics added)."

But, while all societies try to help dependent groups, such help is usually portrayed and perceived as part of a reciprocal exchange. The help is either for services formerly rendered by the dependent donee (or his representatives), or it is in expectation of future counterdonations by the donee. Such reciprocal exchanges pose an especially interesting intellectual question: how is the counterdonation from the dependent donee identified or symbolized? For it is this counterdonation that transforms simple taking into an exchange.

The reciprocal element is necessary because it defines and brakes the flow of donations (or obligations to donate). Without such a constraint, the process of donating would be unmanageable: the wants of dependent donees are potentially limitless. After all, who can say how much love someone wants or "deserves"? And how much care is a disable person "entitled" to? However, in vital societies dependent donees — unless they are bereft of reason — have been socialized to give something back in return for their donations; this sense of obligation moderates their appetites. The moderating effect is especially powerful when the obligation of repayment is directly symbolized — at the time of the donation — through symbolic counterdonations.

For instance, imagine a dependent donee who, following the pre-vailing conventions, displays gratitude and deference when receiving donations. The donee may feel that such profferings are degrading. Indeed, they may obligate him to perform — at some future occasion — onerous favors for the independent donor. Thus, the donee may con-clude he does not want too much help from the donor. And he either moderates his requests or refuses aid. This self-restraint helps define the "needs" of the donee; for, if his needs were really profound, he would offer the appropriate symbolic counterdonations. The refusal to make such an offer signifies "I don't need help so much that I will pay the required price for it."

The norms which require symbolic counterdonations also serve another vital purpose. Obviously, not all independent donors want to donate, even if the appropriate symbolic counterdonations are proffered. Some affluent persons are selfish. But many interactions between in-dependent donors and dependent donees occur in public and semi-public forums. In such instances, where a dependent donee has offered the appropriate deference, public criticism can be directed at the independent donors who "refuse to meet their obligations." Such criticism — which may be directed at the "rich" — does not deprive potential donors of all control of their property. The criticism only says that, in reciprocal situations, those who "have" are obligated to help those who are without. The criticism is not against the wealthy *per se*. Such generalized criticism would destroy all incentives for productivity. Instead, the blame is levied only against those wealthy groups which fail to meet requests for help (a) that are already obliga-tions due through the previous donations of the now dependent donors, or (b) which the potential donees are obviously willing to treat as reciprocal obligations.

As mentioned earlier, exchanges among age-groups are only one form of exchanges among dependent and independent groups. But such exchanges will be an important point of focus in this book. So let us consider this sub-category of exchanges in more detail. But, first a qualification. Age groups do not mean the same thing as generations. Generations suggest groups perhaps twenty years apart. But important exchanges can occur between age groups five or ten years apart (e.g., adolescents can engage in child care), and thus the word "age group" — which includes generations but is wider in its scope — is more accurate.[16] Furthermore, in the text of this book, the word "cohort" will often be applied to designate such groups. Cohort signifies a group of persons who have entered a system at a common point of time: persons born in 1960 are a cohort, as are the students who enrolled in college as freshmen in 1978. Cohort is more encompassing than "age group," and this is helpful, since a society may choose to treat a group who passed a certain point at a specified time as if they were of a common age, even though they were born at different times. If a society follows such a practice, those cohorts are, in effect, age groups. Indeed, it is generally only in literate societies that we have the capability of grouping persons by their age (i.e., the date of their birth). More primitive societies, lacking modern record systems, typically managed age grading by grouping adolescents and adults into cohorts defined in relation to the time they went through some adolescent rite of passage. The times of those occasions were identified and remembered by the participants.

Intercohort Reciprocity

Exchanges among cohorts are one of the most basic exchanges in all societies. Children are obviously helpless and cannot survive or grow without help from older persons. Older adults gradually decline in vitality, and need the assistance and sympathy of younger persons if they are to live their last years in a satisfying fashion. It is true that sometimes older adults retain certain aspects of wealth or power which provide them with security. But the declining physical vigor of the dependent aged, and their status as a numerical minority, means that they cannot retain their wealth or power without the tacit sympathy of the more vigorous majority. In other words, if the vigorous majority began some campaign of expropriation directed against the aged, the aged would lack the vitality to defend themselves. We do not expect such campaigns (though some very poor societies do send their aged out to die) because of a variety of assumptions that preculde us from using raw force to take from a helpless persons (who is aged) something he has fairly earned, and which we thus "owe" him. Exchanges among cohorts can involve individuals or groups of donors or donees. Their subject matter can be tangible (food or money) or intangible (concern and time). The exchange can be immediate (the parent assists the child, and he says "Thank you") or remote (the parent assists the child and, thirty years later, the child supports the parent in his old age). It can be discrete (and have a clearly defined act of donation and counterdonation) or continuous (and involve an almost infinite number of transactions and exchanges between the parties). The exchange can also be direct (the child will later assist the particular adults that helped him) or indirect (the matured child assists a later cohort of children, to "repay" for the donation he received from others as a child). Obligations may be enforced formally (through a lawsuit compelling the child to pay support for his aged parents) or informally (as when the parent or child acts in response to family pressures). Oftentimes, the exchanges rely on mediating agencies.

The most obvious donations to dependent children are tangible: providing them with food, shelter, education or training, and other necessaries. But the value of the intangible resources donated by the family and society (i.e., especially, time and concern) may be even greater than the value of the tangible donations. In other words, the costs of raising a human child are immensely greater than the costs of raising the young of larger mammals. The costs are high because so many adults have to donate much time to socializing a child to become an effective adult in a particular society. In various cultures, these socialization costs to adults are allocated through different means. There can be tax systems, to pay for schools (not that schools, even in modern societies, do most of the "job"). Members of an extended family can share many of these obligations. Ceremonial structures maintained by mediating agencies can play an important part. In small, stable communities, neighbors can informally assist one another in child-care, or societies may design and maintain other systems that do some part or all of the job. But whatever form these systems take, they are costly; wholesome socialization to adulthood is an expensive process. The costs are shared between the parents and society. But there are different ways of dividing the costs, and societies dedicate different proportions (and absolute amounts) of their resources to this task.

The costs to adult society of socializing and nourishing children are, at first, merely donations: they are not automatically exchanges. They never become exchanges unless steps are taken by the collective donors to inculcate, in the dependent young donees, a sense of responsibility and gratitude. Then, the donees will grow into adults who will participate in reciprocal life. For instance, assume a group of adults (now, in 1980, in their thirties) who expect that children, now in the status of dependent donees, will grow up to accept their tangible, remote, continuous, indirect obligations to support cohorts of yet-to-be-born infants and children. In other words, these current adult donors hope that cohorts of contemporary children will be socialized to help society continue through supporting (both as citizens and parents) future children in exchange for the help they are now receiving. Obviously, this "obligation" is highly informal. Thirty years from now in 2010, it will be impractical for some sixty year old to sue the cohort of then thirty year olds, alleging that that cohort was collectively failing to meet its indirect reciprocal obligation to provide an efficient education system for the young. If most of the members of the cohort of thirty year olds do not feel that sense of informal obligation in 2010, it is too late for such a lawsuit. Presumably, the cohort of donors made their mistake in 1980, when they supported the dependent young without properly socializing them to reciprocity.

The need to socialize the young to reciprocity is not only triggered by each adult's vision of his own dependent old age. Most society members also perceive that reciprocity is a vital element of all social life. And so the adults assume that, unless the maturing young are generally indoctrinated to practice reciprocity, a variety of tensions will affect all society members as the cohort matures.

To some degree, the general norms of reciprocity among equals, or toward potent superiors are not too hard to communicate; persons who frequently try to exploit their equals or superiors are usually brought to task. But maintaining a reciprocally oriented attitude toward dependents is another matter. After all, such persons cannot always protect their own interests (or "rights"); as a result, children may be tempted to exploit them. However, as already noted, there are important reasons for societies to advance pro-helping values. Thus, healthy societies generally seek to foster such attitudes. And the diverse structures which assist those ends also powerfully affect the general socialization of the young.

Now, we must again turn from the general to the particular. Assume that groups of adults want to socialize the young to practice reciprocity towards members of other age groups, to justify the donations they are making. Two conceptual questions come to mind: how is this socialization conducted? and who decides what values are inculcated?

Socialization to intercohort reciprocity is managed by first stimulating the child to perceive a network of intercohort reciprocity pervading the society. The child (and future adult) is treated as part of this network. He is informed that, as he matures, he will participate in a number of increasingly larger social systems with diverse patterns of reciprocal intercohort relations. These concepts are first communicated through simple simulations (e.g., the family as a reciprocity system) and symbolic devices. Gradually, the child participates in more complicated situations. He has new symbols revealed or perceives old symbols at more complex levels. This process essentially requires the sympathetic understanding of most of the persons surrounding the child and young adult. They all cooperate to help him interpret the varied information he receives in terms consistent with the overall intent of socialization to intercohort reciprocity. None of this is in conflict with teaching the child to protect his own individual interests. However, such need for protections should be put in the framework of escaping exploitation by "deviant" individuals or groups, and not in one which portrays the general society as hostile.

Who decides what values are inculcated? Theoretically, this decision is made by the persons whose money, time, and energy sustain the dependent child. But this proposition requires qualification. The persons with the power to decide — by choosing to cut off their help if they are not satisfied — must have some vision of what they want done. In other words, a person who donates money to maintain a facility to feed and teach children — with the assumption that it is good to feed and teach children — has the power to decide whether and what kinds of reciprocity that facility will promote. If the donor merely turns the management of that facility over to a "certified" expert, the donor has turned over his socialization power to the expert and his aides. Again, if a donor actively wants to socialize children to reciprocity, that donor must have some concepts that he can use to translate his aspirations into actions and symbols that produces his desired effect. Finally, we must recognize that, in most situations, other agencies are competing with donors to decide what values will be socialized into the child; these agencies realize that, if they determine those values, they can manipulate the child's (or adult's) conduct to their benefit. Unless the donor has some purposeful, active socialization policy, the competing agencies — in the fashion of the Pied Piper — may appropriate the fruits of his efforts.

In sum, if any person or group — whether an individual parent or a vast institution — wants to socialize children to reciprocity, he has to make certain deliberate decisions. Otherwise, personal or institutional selfishness will "naturally" take control. If such selfishness takes control, the child may exploit his family; or it may love the family and exploit society; or exploit his family and love society. Or the child — as he matures — may become so confused by the apparently conflicting reciprocal demands made upon him that he will desperately strive to withdraw from life. (Note: the phrase was "apparently" conflicting demands; whether demands really are conflicting depends, in part, on how we have been socialized to perceive them.) In any case, moving the child through this sequence of enlarging networks is tricky business.

Let me conclude this discussion of reciprocity among dependent and independent groups, and among cohorts in particular, with some specific factors that shape such exchanges. The proportion of independent to dependent persons, and the age distribution in society, are both significant.[17] In other words, how many immediately productive persons are there compared to unproductive persons and how long are unproductive persons encouraged or required to remain unproductive? The allocation of power among independent and dependent groups is also important.[18] Power can be defined in a variety of ways: the physical vitality of different groups; the right to vote; and the varied criteria for allocating status and prestige. The general level of economic productivity must be considered, too: the higher per capital level of productivity, the more resources there are available for independent persons to allocate to dependent persons. A final factor relates to the sense of cohesion enveloping dependent and independent groups. If prevailing circumstances (especially the socialization systems) create powerful loyalties among such groups, then independent donors may make great sacrifices to help dependent

Wiglaf spoke, said many fit words to his companions — his mind was mournful: "I remember that time when we drank mead, when we promised our lord in the mead-hall — him who gave us these gold rings — that we would repay him for his gifts of war-arms if a need like this befell him. Of his own will he chose us among the host for this venture, thought us worthy of fame — and gave me these treasures.... It does not seem right to me for us to bear our shields home again unless we can first fell the foe, defend the life of our prince. I know well it would be no recompense for past deeds that he alone of our tribe should suffer pain, and fall in the fight."

Then he waded through the deadly smoke, bore his war helmet to the aid of his prince...."Beloved Beowulf,...great spirited noble, brave of deed, you must protect your life with all your might. I will help you."

—**Beowulf** (early eighth century)[1]

CHAPTER 2

Reciprocity in Pre-Industrial Cultures

Patterns of reciprocal activities are widespread among many animal societies,[2] and are found in all human societies. From such dispersion, it might be assumed that the patterns are the outcome of innate genetic tendencies.[3] However, it could be difficult to prove that conclusion: all humans and most animals are raised in contact with older members of their species, and it is thus hard to distinguish between learned conduct and innate tendencies. Still, there are examples of social learning shaping the expression of a number of innate traits: for example, sexual and eating patterns vary among societies, but all societies provide means for the gratification of these basic drives.

I hold the position that (a) human beings have a genetic drive to engage in reciprocal activities, and (b) the means through which this drive is expressed are the outcome of social learning and individual genetic variations. Those who disagree with the genetic drive hypothesis may still benefit from the book, since — even if we lack such a reciprocal disposition — the prevalence of reciprocity among all societies means it is a socially important human characteristic.

For tens of thousands of years, man lived in pre-industrial society. The patterns of reciprocity in that society were constrained by primitive technologies and the low level of available scientific knowledge. Still, that society faced many of the reciprocity problems we face today, e.g., it had to sustain and socialize its young and could not routinely ignore responsiblities to its aged. The systems for sustaining reciprocity that developed in this society — as derived from the evidence available to anthropologists and historians — can give us some comprehension of how the apparent human tendencies towards both generosity and selfishness can be shaped to serve society. Of course, one might speculate that the significance of such previous systems may be affected by past and future evolutionary change in human emotional tendencies. Maybe these systems will be irrelevent if we develop a new form of human being. However, geneticists have estimated that given absolute control of a race of human captives for fifteen generations (that is, for three hundred years) — like keeping mice in a cage — they might be able to breed in a new trait or tendency; presumably, without such terrifying power, the trait could take thousands of years to evolve.[4] Obviously, the traits of pre-industrial man are likely to be with us indefinitely. It will, therefore, be helpful to see how these traits were socialized to reciprocity.

The Social Context of Exchanges

The term "pre-industrial cultures" encompasses societies ranging from frontier America to Elizabethan England to classical Greece or Rome, and to small, nomadic tribes of hunters and gatherers. Despite this diversity, there were important common features among many of these cultures that affected their practice of reciprocity. Essentially, the societies lacked elaborate, expeditious recordkeeping systems, or structured, predictable arrangements for adjudication. Thus, while some of these societies used money for the purpose of certain exchanges, even in the semi-monetary societies an overwhelming proportion of their exchanges occurred outside their monetary systems and were governed by informal enforcement procedures. Today, in post-industrial society, a somewhat familiar dichotomy exists: many exchanges occur in the monetary economy, controlled by judicial procedures; but

many other significant exchanges — both monetary and non-monetary — occur among family members or other persons with "trust"
relationships. In such instances, the particpants assume that the obligations created will be enforced through their network of trust.
However, it is also evident that the proportion of monetary exchanges,
when compared to trust exchanges, is much higher in post-industrial
society that it was in earlier societies. In any event, in pre-industrial
societies, informal inforcement procedures were usually effective for
their innumerable exchanges because the parties to the exchanges felt
themselves bound by common systems of sympathy and belief.[5]

These relatively powerful common understandings were sustained
by a variety of factors. In part, they were efficacious because certain
types of goods (e.g., land) were often viewed as incapable of donation
because their donation was contrary to the spirit of reciprocity. Such
constraints simplified the operation of reciprocity networks. But, more
importantly, exchanges were often directly tied to the operation of
powerful systems of ceremony and myth. The reliance on such mediating
systems intensified the power of the enforcement structure. Naturally,
the engagement of these systems also limited the potential participants
in exchanges, since the number and classes of persons who would feel
committed by such ceremonies and myths would naturally be limited.
Therefore, exchanges between comparatively unknown persons, or persons not members of the clan (or equivalent unit) were extremely
limited and perhaps restricted to tangible, immediate, discrete acts
of barter. The effect of these mediating systems was to relate intimately
many interpersonal and intergroup transactions to the psychic life of
the culture.

Karl Polanyi was deeply concerned about this relationship between
material exchanges and cultural vitality. He contended that many societies "recognized" the desirability for basing important human activities, such as material exchanges, on mixed motives (in contrast to the
modern preference for economic relationship based solely on economic
profit.)[6] While social structures that provoke such admixtures of motives
clearly complicate the analysis of exchanges, Polanyi wondered if important, single-purpose economic exchanges (i.e., those made solely
for profit motives) were, perhaps, inherently socially destabilizing,
and ultimately destructive. He analogized these exchanges to marriages

based solely on sex.[7] Without deprecating the importance of material
gain or sex, Polanyi argued that such powerful (but narrow) motivations, lacking the restraints generated by the admixture of other human drives, might assume exaggerated importance for the participants.
By the time the participants recognize their over-commitment to narrow
ends, it may be too late to bring useful remedies into play.

The relationship between exchanges and the psychic life of pre-
industrial societies is demonstrated by donors' frequent sponsorship
of ceremonial feasts, and by the donation of elaborate gifts (to guests)
on such occasions. Sometimes these feasts lasted for several days;
the feasts, and the accompanying donations of gifts, were essentially
forms of economic redistribution. For example, one anthropologist
identified nineteen separate occasions for major feasts among the
Maori of New Zealand.[8] Each of these occasions for donating a feast
(sometimes for hundreds of people) might occur one or more times in
the life of a major leader. The Kwakiutl Indians of Northwest
North America held periodic ceremonial feasts (their famous potlatch),
during which hosts increased their prestige by providing elaborate
feasts and distributions of gifts for their guests, and even at times the
public destruction of part of their wealth, to underline their largesse.[9]
However, the guests (when they were of the same social class as the
host) understood that attendance created a reciprocal obligation for
them to conduct such a redistribution on an equivalent occasion.
When guests were dependents — members of lower status classes —
their attendance obligated them to provide the independent host with
later donations appropriate to their status, e.g., political support,
military service. While the donations to dependents were actually
welfare, or income redistribution, the acceptance of the gifts obligated
the donees to make certain forms of repayment (or the donation was
in recognition of some earlier service by the dependent donee). In
sum, no dependent was soley a taker — a parasite.

The "trades" just described were, in their skeletal form, akin
to modern conventions about adults or families exchanging presents
or visits. And there are obvious parallels. However, in pre-industrial
societies, the ceremonies surrounding the feast and gifts had a profound character for their participants — in contrast to dinner-table
conversation. Furthermore, the comparative scale of distribution of
food and goods was much larger.

The Virtues of Imprecise Equivalence

Of course, such non-monetary systems of redistribution must have created problems with the computation of appropriate reciprocal balances between donors and donees. Exact calculation of the non-monetary donations exchanged as a result of feasts occurring at different times, and with somewhat different participants, was obviously impossible. However, such inexactitude can, in itself, serve a variety of constructive purposes. The provision of elaborate mutual donations is a key characteristic of all persisting human societies. The forms such donations take, and the conditions attached to them, are affected by many material and cultural variables. Still, the practice of indirect reciprocity is essentially the foundation on which donations rest. However, it is impossible to estimate the variety of donations that particular dependent persons may need, and we cannot calculate the amount we will be able to give in return. These impossibilities mean that we cannot precisely determine the amount of reciprocity due to others in future indefinite circumstances. This foreseeable imprecision argues for the existence of systems of inexact reciprocity — so we can be socialized to approach the unpredictable with appropriate flexibility.

Without such a perspective, donors may be tempted to assess how many strokes they should be willing to take in an attempt to rescue a drowning swimmer, or how much money they should be willing to spend in hiring a doctor to save their child, and so on. The application of mechanistic accounting to such situations may well strike us as callous. And, as a practical matter, we suspect that, were such accounting devices available, too many citizens would use them as an excuse to avoid unpleasant and dangerous responsibilities. Thus, the more imprecise the reciprocity system, the broader the responsibilities that can be generated to the benefit of all. Presumably, that is why many pre-industrial societies place such a high premium on honor, loyalty, courage and other evidences of fidelity within their basic group: the assumption is that what the members of such groups "owe" one another is incalculable. And, thus, they all are advantaged because the lack of a precise system discourages calculation.

Apart from matters of urgent and unpredictable need, networks of inexact reciprocity are desirable because most reciprocal obliga-

tions — even quite mundane ones — are not capable of precise calculation. In fact, in our later discussion of modern (especially monetary)
reciprocity systems, we will see that a great deal of artifice and unconscious fiction surrounds many apparently carefully calculated
transactions, and that many exchanges are really inexact.
Reciprocity systems that maintain a degree of obscurity in their transactions are vital. They encourage participants in elaborate exchanges
to devote their psychic energy to productive activities, rather than
fruitless, exhausting calculations about the determination of their
"fair share." To consider a simple analogy: families probably operate
better when all participants have such a high degree of trust that they
assume everyone is working for the good of the whole; conversely,
if each member feels compelled to engage in frequent exacting analyses about how much he is ahead or behind the others, the family
may stop working well for anyone. But such assumptions of reciprocal
trust arise only when all members of the community have been appropriately socialized.

Another significant aspect of a system of inexact reciprocity is
role specialization. The wider, and more vital and diffuse the network
fostering role specialization, the less each participant needs to
feel that he must produce all forms of goods and services
required for survival. As long as a participant is a significant
contributor to some activity, that contribution to the whole entitles him
to counterdonations from other network members. Theoretically, such
specialization should lead to higher productivity. Conversely, if the
cohesion of reciprocal networks begins to decay, participants will feel
a great need to be "self-reliant" and self-contained. In the short run,
this will provide them with a greater security; in the long run, the
overall pool of goods and services will be lessened. We have a
contemporary instance of the decay of such a network. In many
suburban communities, there is a tradition of housewives and mothers
providing the community with voluntary community services. For a
variety of reasons, the reciprocal network (both intracommunity and
intrafamily) in these environments has declined. Thus more of these
former volunteer workers are seeking paid employment — to become
self-reliant. As a result, one form of specialized service — the volunteer community worker — is less available. Either the void is not

filled, or it is filled by the expansion of paid employees, e.g., social workers and school aides. Regardless of the institutional response to the void, it is probable that the volunteers provided "better" services than those available after the systemic change. In sum, suburban housewives "worked" both before and after the increase of paid female employment; but their earlier system of "working" — or making donations — was reinforced through inexact counterdonations of affection, regard, and role-gratification; their current donations are repaid with money — a more precise form of counterdonation. Later, I will argue that volunteer community workers are essentially more "productive" than paid professionals; but accepting this argument requires us to develop different performance criteria than those typically proposed by the professionals.

Still another noteworthy characteristic of pre-industrial societies that relates to reciprocity is their perspective on the concept of "rights." Citizens did have rights, and there were usually means of enforcement. However, rights were typically seen as integrated parts of a whole which also included duties and entitlements; while different parts received emphasis at different times, the integrated nature of the whole was always kept in the forefront. In effect, just as such societies discouraged single-purpose exchanges, they also discouraged highly constrained interpretations of rights.

Ceremony, Myths, and Reciprocity

The relationship between the mythic and ceremonial life of pre-industrial societies and their reciprocity systems invites extended discussion. This relationship means that, in such societies, families — and cultures comprised of families — understood that serious exchanges could not continue to occur unless their children were socialized to accept mediating myths and ceremonies. These myths and ceremonies were the equivalent of our contemporary systems of taxation, bookkeeping, business, law, and government. Of course, the objectives of the mediating systems of myth and ceremony differ somewhat from those applied in modern systems. The persons who managed systems of myth and ceremony were not only concerned with increasing the variety, quantity, and richness of exchanges; they were equally concerned with maintaining social stability, and with providing their believers with psychic satisfaction. Thus, the mythic, ceremonial, and reciprocal patterns of such societies reinforced each other. We might consider a still-persisting modern example of such reinforcement: a religious wedding ceremony. Theologically, the ceremony asks the blessing of God on the venture of the couple; simultaneously, it hallows an intangible, remote, direct, continuing exchange (the couple's marriage) that is subject to both informal and formal enforcement. We can see that the ceremony might tend to improve the quality of the marriage, because it clearly demarcates a moment of passage, and thus intensifies the psychic life of the couple. Similarly, the ceremonial and mythic patterns of the general society are enriched by an act which ties such patterns to a vital moment of human life. When the marriage is hallowed by a religious ceremony, the partners are often members of the same religion (and, indeed, some religions enforce this homogeneity as a requirement for the ceremony). When the homogeneity exists, the partners have been socialized to see the ceremony, and its implications, from a common perspective. Thus, the efficacy of the ceremony is intensified. In pre-industrial cultures, equivalent ceremonies might have surrounded the "purchase" or "sale" of cattle, weapons, ships, or services, or the delivery of payments equivalent to taxes.

Socialization to vigorous common beliefs becomes increasingly challenging if the class of persons to be socialized is widely dispersed, and/or encompass a large number of people. Conversely, the more time that is spent in creating and maintaining such socialization, through collective participation in ceremonies, the popular reiteration of myths and so on, the wider the network of belief that can be sustained. For example, during the Middle Ages, the Catholic Church was a powerful international mediating system — and the Church celebrated over a hundred holy days (i.e., holidays) apart from Sundays. In modern times, in Nazi Germany, when Hitler and his supporters sought to build up pro-Nazi spirit, millions of citizens were enlisted in rallies, parades, and other ceremonial activities. In both instances, elaborate time- and resource-consuming activities socialized large numbers of persons to identify with the beliefs of the mediating systems. The larger the reciprocity network to be sustained, the more time must be spent in creating "emotional cement" — unless a powerful totalitarian system (e.g., the Soviet Union) chooses to attain the same end partly by keeping out distracting forces. Obviously, all such systems of potent common belief provided their members with many satisfactions beyond facilitating material transactions.

Voluntarism: A Misleading Concept

Vital systems of informal enforcement often create an aura of voluntarism around reciprocal obligations.[10] Indeed, some social scientists have given preferred status to donations stimulated by voluntary or altruistic motives.

In many exchanges, there is an appearance of voluntarism. However, we misread the situation if we accept this appearance for reality. The terms "voluntary" and "altruistic" mean donating (or giving counterdonations) without the pressure of threats, the expectation of repayments, or the hope of praise, gratitude, or deference. Praise, gratitude, and deference should be seen as forms of counterdonations, since (a) they are often pleasing to donors in themselves, and (b) they symbolize obligations which can be translated into tangible counterdonations.

Thus, on closer examination, most donations we call altruistic are motivated by reciprocal considerations. In fact, even the popularization of the word "altruistic" (to characterize some donors) is a form of counterdonation — for surely a person popularly regarded as altruistic can feel entitled to deference.

Of course, alternative definitions could be developed. For example, we could simply equate voluntarism with choice, *per se*. Then, any donation made by someone with the formal power to refuse to donate would be a voluntary act. But such a definition is so broad as to be useless. People almost always have choices; the issue is the costs involved in exercising a particular choice. We do not have to pay our taxes — we can choose to go to jail, like Thoreau; if someone offers a poor man an immense bribe to perform some minor act, he can choose to continue to live in poverty; and, if we do not like our jobs, we are not slaves and literally compelled to keep them. When someone says he has no choice, he usually means he is choosing an easy alternative rather than a hard one. Thus, if we want to attribute some metaphysical virtue to persons who choose to make donations, we should assume they have no incentive to make an appropriate choice, e.g., to render benefit to another. Eventually, such do-gooders would have to use some random number system to allocate their donations in order to insure that their choices are not affected by subconscious elements of self-interest. It is difficult to imagine what forms of human relations would prevail in environments which apply such randomizing principles; whatever the image we conceptualize, it does not leave one feeling at ease.

Despite these intellectual anomalies, there is a certain seductive appeal in the concept of voluntary or altruistic donations. This appeal must be recognized, or we will be unable to appreciate fully some of the important attitudes and motives shaping our views about reciprocity. The theme of voluntary benevolence will reappear later when we describe the development of reciprocity involving independent and dependent groups in Western society.

From the viewpoint of many donees, purely altruistic donations would be quite desirable; altruism would mean the donee was under no obligation to offer counterdonations.Indeed if donees frequently offered spontaneous counterdonations, the donations would become less altruistic, since the potential donors might be motivated in their giving by the perception that donees usually returned counterdonations. Thus, we can expect that some articulate potential donees will praise "true" altruism. Another group possibly attracted by the goal of altrusim are persons given the onerous assignment of socializing the young (and others) to practice gratitude, e.g., the repayment of obligations. Earlier, I suggested this is hard work for many socializers. But, if altruism is a supreme value, the young should not bother with gratitude, since frequent sincere gratitude is inconsistent with altruism. Finally, the aspiration to make altruistic giving a common mode of human conduct implies that human beings possess an extraordinarily high level of potential generosity. Consider the nobility of the idea: that many humans can give for long periods of time without any expectation of gratitude, reward, or recognition! Perhaps this semi-utopian potential appeals to some people. Others may find it a bit repugnant or grotesque — or at least prone to distortion and exploitation.

It is true that many reciprocity systems strive to maintain an appearance of voluntarism — which is partly what informal enforcement is about. But, even with informal enforcement, repayment usually occurs because the donees simply meet the norms of the community in which they have spent their lives. And, in practice, donors act on this assumption. In a philosophical sense, it is difficult to say whether such acts are involuntary or voluntary: they are involuntary because persistent rejection of the norms of tightly knit communities can eventually subject us to severe penalties, ranging from loneliness to exile and dealth; they are voluntary because some norms can be rejected with low cost and, if we can "afford" exile, we can choose to escape the entire demand.

We will be more precise if we abandon the use of the word "voluntary" in any literal sense, and merely say that informal enforcement networks (a) create a greater *appearance* of voluntariness, and (b) subject donees (in minor matters) to only modest pressures to reciprocate. In any event, even the appearance of voluntariness is significant. That appearance entitles donees who reciprocate to the respect and gratitude of others for their pro-social "choice" — and such attention is inherently satisfying. Indeed, even when that attention is not overtly granted, the repaying donees may feel a sense of self-regard because of their display of generosity. Of course, one purpose of the mediating systems for informal enforcement that we have been discussing is to stimulate such displays of respect and gratitude among donors and donees, and to encourage them to feel pride in their conduct. In contrast, formal enforcement systems dedicate their energies to reminding prospective donors that if they do not pay (their taxes, for example), they will be subject to automatic penalties. And, of course, such systems also apply equivalent impersonal punitive procedures to donees who do not satisfy their reciprocal obligations. There are obvious "social economies" attached to formal enforcement — displaying respect and gratitude is often time-consuming. To apply more dramatic terminology, we might also mention that many modern donees also find such expectations — that they display obvious gratitude to donors — humiliating. It may, therefore, seem easier for donees (and their allies) to threaten potential donors with jail or seizure of their possessions than to grant them deference, e.g., to say seriously and sincerely "Thank you" or "Please." But, as we will see, enforcement by explicit threats can also be socially expensive.

Making Informal Enforcement Work

In order to work effectively, informal enforcement requires the engagement of many community members. This is one reason why it needs strong socialization systems. The engagement is reflected in the praise and respect which community members deliver to responsible donors and donees. It is reflected in the criticism and obloquies that are directed at irresponsible and selfish donors and donees (and it is not always comfortable to proffer serious and open criticism). Finally, it is reflected in the attention which community members direct towards the conduct of one another in order to judge whether that conduct is praiseworthy. Inevitably, there will be ambiguous norms about certain forms of reciprocal conduct, and this process of observation and judgment will sometimes evolve into a system of deliberate evaluation. Frequently, such evaluations are considered and articulated by mediating systems: and they may even take profoundly artistic forms, such as the moral issues weighed in the plays of Sophocles or Shakespeare.

This whole process of evaluation consumes time and emotional energy, and has some inherent inexactitude — and potential for abuse. We can recognize the pejorative terms by which monitoring conduct can be characterized: gossip, prying, nosiness. However, the other extreme is a social environment in which a person neither pays attention to what others do, nor forms any opinion about it. In such an environment, all observations and requirements for evaluation are turned over to the courts, the police, and other formally designated persons. Of course, such highly formalistic social environments — pervaded as they are with human indifference to individuals — do exist: subway trains, city streets crowded with pedestrians. However, we must also understand that persisting indifference among persons who must stay in close touch with one another is a symptom of social disintegration.[11] So the close attention and judgment of others — despite the tension such engagement inevitably generates — is a concomitant of vital social life. Those who are interested in our conduct and disapprove of it are "busybodies"; those who are interested and approve are "friends." But who is to say our conduct always deserves approval?

There is another element that affected the flow of help from independent to dependent persons in pre-industrial environments. On the whole, the independent persons were helping dependent persons they personally knew — their own kinsmen, serfs, or fellow villagers. This intimacy permitted the donor to assess carefully the donee's situation. Indeed, when unknown donees solicited help, it was expected that they have some obvious plausible sign of their dependency. Thus, medieval beggars were persons who were deformed or maimed (or who assumed such disguises). These visible signs assured potential independent donors that such unknown supplicants were in "genuine" need.

The involvement of much of the community in the informal enforcement of reciprocal obligations creates peculiar emotional demands on citizens. They are expected to act concurrently as judges, friends, admirers, and critics of others, and to assume their co-citizens will display similar attitudes towards them. Inevitably, in this process, they will be tempted to see particular community members in predetermined perspectives (i.e., to apply stereotypes and rely on the criterion of social status) to escape the burden of making endless segmented judgments. Still, important or prosperous community members cannot escape the final obligation of occasionally making "objective" judgments, for if such judgments are widely avoided, significant persons may be seriously victimized. Social environments in which such judgments are frequently demanded can stimulate the growth of personal characteristics such as tact, patience, and skill at listening to, assessing, and communicating subtle ideas. Of course, this interpersonal process will be interwoven with the mythic and ceremonial values of each particular community, and those values will be alien to an outsider. Still, the basic interpersonal skills involved are relatively generalizable. Perhaps these are the skills that have stimulated many Western observers of primitive leaders to remark on their dignity and evident grace.[12] These traits are the external evidence of the emotional characteristics we have been discussing.

Status and Reciprocity

Henry Maine, in 1861, characterized pre-industrial reciprocity as based on status rather than contract.[13] His portrayal accurately described many aspects of such societies, where citizens were socialized to assume continuing intergroup and intragroup obligations without reliance on formal enforcement. Inevitably, a citizen's status in such societies was defined by these often predetermined obligations. Each person had an evident ascribed (or even earned) status, which reminded him and informed others of the reciprocal expectations that surrounded him. While these expectations might be elaborate, socialization to such knowledge was still feasible because each status had its own particular integrated expectations. In addition, reciprocal obligations even among persons who did not know each other were clarified by the norms of status — speaking humorously, in one era, knights knew they were expected to rescue maidens in distress or abandon the desirable status of being a knight; the maidens, of course, had concomitant obligations. Maine contrasted such patterns with the increasing emphasis on formal, discrete, contractual reciprocity, which was the trend in the English society of his time. In such contractual situations, the participants played a large part in deliberately shaping their own roles.

Community members can participate in informal enforcement only if the general community routinely assumes that intracommunity reciprocity is a basic obligation — that the exchange of "favors" should be the norm. While industrial and post-industrial adults — as well as primitive peoples — all tend to accept that persepctive, there is apparently a qualitative difference between the prevailing attitudes toward reciprocity in pre-industrial and modern societies. Many major thinkers in literate, but pre-industrial societies — Aristotle, Seneca, Cicero — composed serious treatises on the duty of reciprocity.[14] The view typically presented was that the distribution of gifts and favors was an obligation of persons with status and that the dependent donees of such gifts — who were members of the independent donors' class, tribe or community — were obligated to return those donations. The dependent donees were often described as the donors' "clients." Such participation in reciprocity was an act consonant with being human. The following remarks from Seneca reflect the spirit with which many classic philosophers approach reciprocity and one of its central elements, gratitude:

> Ingratitude is something to be avoided in itself
> because there is nothing that so effectively disrupts

and destroys the harmony of the human race as this vice. For how else do we live in security if it is not that we help each other by the exchange of good offices? It is only through the interchange of benefits that life becomes in some measure equipped and fortified against sudden disasters. Take us singly, and what are we? The prey of all creatures, their victims, whose blood is most delectable.... God has given man two things, reason and fellowship, which transform him from being a creature at the mercy of others, into the most powerful creature of all; and so he who, if he were isolated, could be a match for none is the master of the world. Fellowship has given him dominion over all creatures.[15]

Later, in the Christian era, Western explorers, visiting pre-industrial tribes, often experienced difficulty with the concept of the obligations of the donees: such visitors sometimes naively accepted gifts from natives, and then were surprised when the natives casually appropriated any property of the visitors that struck their interest.[16] Their writings made frequent reference to the widespread thievery of the natives. But, to the natives, acceptance of their gifts gave them a license to take what they chose.

For the Classic Greeks, the obverse of reciprocity was "philanthropic" conduct. Philanthropy is "love of man" and encompasses acts undertaken out of selfless affection. Originally, philanthropy was used to describe conduct attributed to the gods, personages of such exhalted status that they could donate without asking for reciprocity (although in most cultures, include Greece, the gods are often portrayed as jealous).[17] In any event, man was not expected to emulate the gods. While various religions have emphasize the obligations of believers (i.e., community members) to give to fellow-believers in distress, this obligation was usually placed in the framework of a community in which all members had reciprocal obligations. The religion simply was one of the mediating agencies that structured these apparently "philanthropic" transactions. In Western cultures, the doctrines of early Christiantity reinforced traditional attitudes towards

reciprocity. These doctrines typically stressed the mutual (i.e., reciprocal) obligations between parents and children, as well as the duty
of the society to assist the ill, aged, and unfortunate. However,
such general aid was often placed in a reciprocal framework. Thus,
medieval scholars commented on the importance of relating the
giving of aid — which involved the distribution of a limited resource —
to the "deservingness" of the dependent donees.[18] The New Testament also usually placed the Christian duty of charity in a reciprocal
framework. For instance, here is one famous section of the Bible
describing the Last Judgment:

> Then shall the King say unto them on his right
> hand, Come, ye blessed of my Father, inherit
> the kingdom prepared for you from the founda-
> tion of the world:
>
> For I was hungered, and ye gave me meat: I
> was thirsty, and ye gave me drink: I was a stranger,
> and ye took me in:
>
> Naked, and ye clothed me: I was sick, and ye
> visited me: I was in prison, and ye came unto me.
>
> Then shall the righteous answer him, saying,
> Lord when saw we thee hungered, and fed thee?
> Or thirsty and gave thee drink?
>
> When saw we thee a stranger, and took thee in?
> Or naked, and clothed thee?
>
> Or when saw we thee sick, or in prison, and
> came unto thee?
>
> And the King shall answer and say unto them,
> Verily I say unto you, inasmuch as ye have done
> it unto one of the least of these my brethren,
> ye have done unto me.
>
> Then shall he say also unto them on the left
> hand, Depart from me, ye cursed, into everlasting
> fire, prepared for the devil and his angels:
>
> Then shall he say also unto them on the left
> hand. Depart from me, ye cursed, into everlasting
> fire, prepared for the devil and his angels:

> For I was hungered, and ye gave me no meat:
> I was thirsty and ye gave me no drink:
>
> I was a stranger, and ye took me not in:
> naked and ye clothed me not: sick, and in prison,
> and ye visited me not.
>
> Then shall they also answer him, saying, Lord,
> when saw we thee hungered, or athirst, or a
> stranger, or naked, or sick, or in prison, and did
> not minister unto thee?
>
> Then shall he answer them, saying, Verily I say
> unto you, Inasmuch as ye did it not unto one of
> the least of these, ye did it not to me.[19]

The explicity attention which most pre-industrial societies gave to the obligation of reciprocity was founded on an essentially tragic view of human nature. They did not assume that man, on his own, would "naturally" meet his social obligations. Without the guidance of his society, he might well tend toward gross selfishness.[20] Implicitly, persons who made donations without maintaining reciprocal frameworks could well be doing a disservice to mankind, since they might be "training" the recipient away from reciprocity. Such training would be destructive to both the individual and the social whole. Indeed, reciprocity, far from creating burdens for man, was finally seen as the way man could attain some degree of power over other persons and events. Precisely because the donation of wealth created obligations for the dependent donees, wealth had significance. Without the expectation of reciprocity from others, man was helpless to affect social life. In fact, pre-industrial man attributed a similarly reciprocal approach to the gods — sacrifices were offered with the hope they would be "accepted." Thus, man's relationship with the gods was not entirely one of subordination; he could make offers to the gods, and hope for reciprocal donations. Man only became powerless when he gave without expectation of any return, or when he caused others to believe they could take without reciprocating.

In the discussion thus far we have neglected to draw a distinction between urban and rural pre-industrial societies. Such a distinction may be appropriate. Urban environments were more likely to include persons who had left their family of birth, and to give greater emphasis to monetary transactions, and to *deliberately* form systems for tangible and intangible, remote, continuous, indirect reciprocity that was (essentially) informally enforced. In other words, the value of flexible systems of reciprocity was still recognized, but new alliances had to be created to replace the kin groups and tribal networks that existed in rural environments. The medieval craft guild is a typical example of such a deliberate mediating system.[21] It is true that the relationships between the guild and "outsiders" were affected by a monetary economy. However, exchanges between guild members were still determined by the criterion of status, and were frequently structured by ceremonial and mythic approaches.

Intercohort Reciprocity

The general elements of pre-industrial reciprocity systems outlined above have dealt, to a large degree, with the relationship between independent and dependent participants in exchanges. While we have given little attention to exchanges specifically among cohorts, the same principles have applicability to such exchanges. Intercohort reciprocity in pre-industrial society was affected by such factors as: the largely non-monetary nature of such exchanges; the use of mythic and ceremonial mediating systems; inexact exchanges; prolonged and explicit socialization to reciprocity; the reliance on status as a socializing device; the immediate nature of many exchanges; the appearance of voluntarism; and the reliance on informal enforcement. Beyond these important general elements, however, there are certain factors that especially relate to intercohort exchanges.

S. N. Eisenstadt presented a highly pertinent model of mediating structures for such exchanges.[22] He proposed that societies could be divided into two categories: universal and parochial. The categorization was derived from the dichotomous relationships between matured children and their parents and families that usually existed in the two types of societies. In universalistic societies, the children, when young, understand that their success in adult life will not be highly dependent on the continuing support of their families, while in parochial societies, persisting family relationships are vital. Modern societies are almost always universalistic, and many (but not all) pre-industrial societies were parochial. Each category of society has the need to socialize the young to its intercohort reciprocity system. But, in universalistic societies, many of the donations to be repaid by the matured young are indirect and mediated by the society, while in parochial societies, a higher proportion of the donations are direct, and are to be repaid to their family (which is often an extended family).

In universalistic societies, young people tend to develop greater identification with their peer group than in parochial societies. This occurs partly because there are fewer incentives for the young to identify with their parents, since their adult life would only be modestly tied with their parents — and they might well continue to have significant adult relations with their peers. Furthermore, in universalistic societies, the young — when they become adults — are expected to participate in society-wide intercohort exchanges (as compared to the family-wide intercohort exchanges typical of parochial societies). In order to socialize youths and adolescents to think in terms of such society-wide obligations, adults in universalistic societies encourage age-grouping, and use those groups as mediating systems to train the young for their adult reciprocal relationships. In other words, their youth age-groups are essentially designed and managed under adult supervision. They are also engaged in routine exchanges with the community, which are prototypes of their later (and more substantial) adult obligations. The adults "design and manage" the age-group by defining the membership of groups through public ceremonies — as the members grow older, periodic ceremonies mark the group's transition to successively mature statuses — and by allocating public service responsiblities to each age-group (e.g., the Cub Scouts, Boy Scouts, and Explorer Scouts in our society). Obviously, the ceremonies could evocatively portray the successful completion of the group's formal responsibilities, and the elevation of its members to more important challenges.

Young cohorts might have minor chores assigned to them — cleaning the village or bringing the water — while older ones might be assigned to military duty. The adults further provide that the successive cohort groups have responsiblities to, and some authority over, one another. Sometimes, members of a cohort group choose their own leader. Still, the framework of general adult supervision operates to insure that the groups satisfy their assigned responsiblities.[23] The incremental increase in the responsibilities assigned to groups as their members age means that their level of "power" is consonant with their age and experience. The sum effect of this process in universalistic societies is to rear cohorts of adults who assume they will engage in exchanges with older and younger cohorts, and who will be prepared to participate actively in the government of the society, even as they had earlier participated in their own governance.

Intercohort reciprocity in pre-industrial society was affected by factors beyond those outlined by Eisenstadt. For instance, such exchanges were necessarily shaped by the prevailing systems of production. In pre-industrial societies, young persons could participate relatively quickly in productive activities. One anthropologist, who studied a contemporary farming village in Indonesia, concluded that peasant children would equal approximately adult levels of production between the ages of six to nine.[24] Of course, there were some adult tasks such children could not yet handle. Still, they could manage certain chores with adult efficiency, and there were enough of these chores around a farm so that the children could be doing full-time adult-type labor. These data mean that children in most pre-industrial communities quickly became engaged in making substantial continuing reciprocal donations and that, conversely, parents did not need to wait many years before their own donations began to be reciprocated.

Counterdonations by the Aged

Older adults in pre-industrial societies (who might be "retired" in industrial societies) continued to make material contributions through day-to-day work, because pre-industrial production systems often used flexible working schedules, or permitted workers with declining vitality to shift to part-time employment. Indeed, the status of a "retired person" — a healthy adult not engaged in productive work — hardly existed in pre-industrial societies. As a person aged, the tempo of his work might decline, but work would only stop in the event of a serious illness or dramatic disability (one that would probably lead to death).

The production systems of a society are also incidentally connected to its means of collecting and controlling the use of wealth, and such means can affect the status of the aged. In stable agricultural societies, land ownership might tend to be concentrated among the aged. In hunting societies, physical vigor might be the most important means of maintaining wealth. In effect, different property structures make it more or less likely that the aged will continue to make donations or have less need for them (as opposed to being dependent on repayments for their earlier remote donations).

But the counterdonations of older persons of diminished vigor in pre-industrial societies went beyond producing material goods or accepting simple responsibilities for caretaking. The old also usually possessed a body of knowledge that could be "donated" for social purposes; they could act as advisors. The "value" of that donation depended on the nature of the society, and its means of organizing and using knowledge. The more any society relied on an oral tradition, the greater the status that could be given to the knowledge donated by the aged. Older people had simply been able to spend more time acquiring such knowledge. Of course, in literate societies, older persons can also disseminate information collected from books, but those books are equally available to the young and old.

The definition of "knowledge" popularly applied throughout the society can also affect the status of the aged (and the young, too). On one hand, knowledge can be defined as the understanding of the motives and attitudes that drive human conduct in general, and the conduct of ourselves and specific others in particular. Such knowledge can be used to forecast and shape human actvities. This type of human-relations knowledge is largely acquired through experience which brings us into extended and intensive contact with other persons.[26] It is the "knowledge" possessed by someone who has reared a child, as opposed to the knowledge of someone who has taken a course on child-rearing. It is knowledge largely acquired through aging. Knowledge can also be defined as cognitive knowledge: the acquiring of discrete, concrete pieces of information, and the concepts and techniques appropriate to manipulate and analyze such data. Cognitive knowledge is largely learned through formal training, under the supervision of experts. It tends to become obsolete comparatively rapidly, since formal training systems and the reliance on experts stimulates the steady creation of new data and techniques. Pre-industrial societies obviously gave preeminence to human-relations knowledge.

The entertainment systems of societies are related to their knowledge structures and can also determine the donations of the aged.

"Entertainment" sounds like a trivial word. But it actually covers all we are doing when we are not working or sleeping. In pre-industrial societies, most of this time was filled with the exchange of gossip, folk tales, myths, and jokes, and the preparation and presentation of ceremonies. Much of this material was also implicitly classified as "wisdom." Obviously, older persons might make significant contributions to such activities, and as a result, their company might be viewed as desirable.

Another intercultural distinction related to traditions of knowing (and affecting the status of the aged) is whether the society has a cyclic or progressive view of time. A cyclic view gives more prominent roles to persons with previous experience, since problems and opportunities will presumably reappear as in the past, and first-hand knowledge of the past is thus valuable. A progressive view assumes that the problems and opportunities of the future will have significant elements of novelty, and that the most precious characteristics in dealing with such events are energy, optimism, and the most recent knowledge. These characteristics are more likely to be found in the young. There is no final answer as to whether the cyclic or progressive view of time is more "correct." Arguments can be made on either side. But it is evident that pre-industrial societies emphasized cyclic perspectives, and thus gave prominence to the particular donations of the aged.

Elements Affecting Intercohort Exchanges

The level of affluence in a society or a social class affects exchanges among cohorts. If the level is high, there are more goods available for donations. But the effects of affluence — or comparative poverty — are quite complicated. Comparative poverty can mean that the society will demand early reciprocity from the young and continue to expect reciprocity from the old. Thus, poverty may simplify the process of socializing the young to reciprocity — especially via tangible, immediate exchanges — and may require the old to keep providing some counterdonations or be abandoned. Of course, many pre-industrial societies were quite poor. Conversely, "prosperity" tends to attenuate exchanges. Producers, in prosperous environments, can afford to support dependent persons for long periods of time without being materially pressured to require counterdonations. Such attenuation is not entirely beneficial. For example, it means that young persons do not have clear instances of the exchange process surrounding them. This can complicate the goal of socialization to reciprocity.

The age distribution in the society is also relevant, as reflected in the so-called dependency ratio: the number of adults of working age, compared to the number of young children and retired persons. The dependency ratio is affected by many factors, e.g., the birth and death rate, the average life-span of persons who attain (let us say) the age of ten years old. Pre-industrial societies typically had very high birth rates and infant death rates and, generally, short life-spans. Thus, the average life-span in ancient Rome and medieval Europe was estimated to be between 20-30 years; by the mid-nineteenth century, it was about 40 years in the United States.[27] Even after one had passed infancy, in earlier societies, the average life-span was still much shorter than is the case today. Data from a number of medieval Hungarian communities disclosed that for persons who had attained the age of 20, their age at death would average 46.[28] As a result, the proportion of "older" persons in earlier populations was not as high as in moderns societies; an estimated 18% of persons born in the United States between 1810-1840 survived to the age of 60 or beyond; fifty years later, the comparable figure was 26%. Indeed, the historic demographic data suggest that the image of grandparents, parents, and children living together under the same roof actually occurred infrequently; the average life-span was so short that only small proportions of adults survived long enough to be grandparents.[29] However, the demographic data must be qualified in some particulars.

An extended family is not only extended "vertically" — through grandparents, parents and children — but also horizontally and diagonally — through cousins, uncles and aunts, and other relationships of blood and marriage. In small, comparatively stable communities, children would be surrounded with many older and younger relatives, even if the "depth" of their vertical relations was comparatively shallow. We should also realize that many middle-aged persons in pre-industrial societies suffered from physical disabilities that made them dependent on their families and communities during what we now would expect to be their hale middle-age. It is difficult to estimate the proportion of such persons from available data. But, surely, many forms of disease, infection, and crippling injuries were more prevalent in the past than in our time.

The geographic stability of a society can also affect its intercohort transactions. Geographically mobile societies (excluding nomadic societies, where the tribe moves in toto) will tend to be universalistic cultures, as the term was defined by Eisenstadt. That is, young persons, who may move away from their families, will be socialized to owe their obligations to the whole society — as compared to their families — and the whole society will have greater a role in their upbringing.

Finally, the role of warfare in the life of the society — that is, if the society is warlike, or if it is seriously concerned with mobilizing for its own defense — shapes the nature of intercohort exchanges. When warfare is significant, comparatively young males will be asked to make very important donations by becoming warriors. They may even be asked to contribute their lives. In such situations, the society will strive to socialize its young to be willing to make such donations — and thus to reciprocate the benefits its young have acquired through the sacrifices of previous (living and dead) youth cohorts. Conversely, in less war-structured societies, the society can "afford" to place less emphasis on such teaching for its young.

Human Feelings in the Past

The medley of elements we have sketched affecting intercohort exchanges formed the substance of human societies for many thousands of years. In some ways, one might say that their persistence, and their regular appearance in widely dispersed societies, is potent evidence of certain inherent traits in human nature. As we will see, signs of the decay of these elements began to appear in Western Europe about the late Middle Ages. We will later discuss these patterns of change. But, at this moment, it will be useful to abandon our concern with reciprocity, and present a general model of the characteristics of the societies we have been describing.

These societies had relatively stable systems of production and social relations. They tended to be geographically constrained. Even when larger systems of communication and authority existed, smaller, relatively cohesive social entities persisted as viable subsystems. The quality of human relations within these societies was intense, though individual persons were in touch with fewer persons throughout their lives than would be the case today. The level of material possessions was relatively low, though persons in an essentially dependent status were viewed as entitled to assistance from their immediate fellow citizens. The quality of cognitive knowledge was low, and there was little understanding of scientific concepts; however, many citizens, especially at higher social levels, had a comparatively sophisticated appreciation of subtle aspects of human relations. The infant death rate was high, and the average life-span of persons who grew to maturity was about 30 years. Relations with "foreign" societies, where there often was not a common framework to sustain reciprocity, were awkward, and tension and intermittant warfare between such societies was common; however, due to the low level of military technology, the death rate in such wars was often low. Philosophically, human nature was viewed as essentially unchangeable, though superior persons might occasionally arise. But it was the demand of the collective that brought out the best elements of man's nature.

Persons who did attain old age continued to make significant counterdonations to these societies and (in the absence of extraordinary poverty in the culture) they were given appropriate recognition for such contributions. Children and youths were quickly enlisted in providing assistance to their families and/or the larger society. Even in affluent, higher status families, children, from an early age were asked to fulfill a variety of dynastic and extended family obligations, or assigned the responsibilities of estate management. While these activities did not constitute manual "work," they often were emotionally demanding. Adults and older children spent high proportions of their time in contact with the young, under circumstances which fostered their socialization to reciprocity. The ceremonies, myths, and symbols of the society were integrated into their transactional life and socialization systems so as to make the activities mutually supportive. And a great deal of time and energy was dedicated to maintaining this integration.

One might wonder if the members of these pre-industrial societies were "happy," or "happier" than persons in more modern societies. The *objective* fact is that they were probably not as happy. According to survey research, the direct answers of respondents living in comparatively primitive contemporary societies (to the question: "Are you happy?") have consistently demonstrated lower levels of "happiness" than better educated, more prosperous respondents in modern societies.[30] However, the very question of "happiness" implies a certain — and comparatively modern — perspective on human relations. Likewise, the question deemphasizes the significance of other important elements of human life. Essentially, happiness is a relatively individualistic value: it implies the possession of material goods, and health, and *perhaps* the maintenance of satisfactory relationships with one's most immediate family. Both industrial and post-industrial societies are largely dedicated to providing citizens with these benefits: we pursue happiness. Wealthy and better-educated citizens in these societies have made large emotional investments to attain that end. However, in lieu of personal happiness, other measures of social efficacy might be proposed. Citizens might be asked, "Do you feel a sense of support from the persons around them?" or "How often have you laughed or cried with your fellows over common concerns?" or "Have you ever helped to produce anything wonderful?" or "How many persons would cry if you died?" We cannot predict that the answers to these questions would correlate positively with the answers about happiness, but it is hard to say which questions are more valid tests of social efficacy. It is not hard to forecast that mature citizens who live in societies that make a great to-do about the pursuit of happiness, and who, personally, dedicate enormous resources to that pursuit, may tell casual questioners that they are happy and imply that the matter of social efficacy is settled.

The model of pre-industrial societies has a certain beneficent tone. But we cannot ignore some of its disturbing implications. The high level of integration within these societies impeded the development of cognitive knowledge: any intellectual change had to be assessed in the light of its relationship to the total life of the society. This assessment inevitably inhibited the development of objective science. Such objectivity would be alien to integration; it would seem just as grotesque as the concept of a major exchange that was judged primarily from an economic perspective.

Eventually, the collective impact of dynamic scientific thought, the attractions of material possessions, and the desire for a prolonged life all gradually eroded this elaborately integrated structure. We will later discuss this process of erosion. However, as citizens of our times, our basic intellectual expectations about intercohort exchanges have been highly colored by the social disintegration inherent in much of modern life. We are inevitably prone to assume that whatever has been around us for most of our own lives (though it is not around all Americans) is natural or typical. But, in reflecting about contemporary exchanges among cohorts, it will be productive to remember that perhaps 95% of all human generations have been born, have lived, and have died in the highly integrated societies we have been describing. An appreciation of what was typical in those societies may help us identify whatever we dare to call the natural tendencies in human beings. Indeed, when we look closely at our own times, we can recognize significant efforts to recreate much of the integration that was destroyed in our pursuits of knowledge, wealth, and longevity. But these efforts have been hampered by our inadequate understanding of the nature of reciprocity in the past. Perhaps that misunderstanding can be rectified.

And now, let us shift our concerns to another important exchange among independent and dependent groups: exchanges that occur among living, dead, and yet-to-be-born cohorts. As we will see, such exchanges have important implications for health and social order.

The belief relative to the dead, and to the worship that was due them, founded the ancient family, and gave it the greater part of its rules....man, after death, was reputed a happy and devine being, but on the condition that the living continued to offer him the funeral repasts....

This opinion was the fundamental principle of domestic law among the ancients. From it followed, in the first place, this rule, that every family must perpetuate itself forever.

— Fustel de Coulanges[1]

CHAPTER 3

The Great Exchange

First, we should consider two theorems:

***Most acts by either individuals or organizations are largely determined by their expectations about the future;

***Those expectations, themselves, are structured by our past learning.

In other words, the teacher teaching a class, the parent feeding a child, or the society participating (through its representatives) in diplomatic negotiations all base their conduct on expectations founded on previously acquired knowledge. This "previous knowledge" may be based on their own personal experience or on information from others. And, the more our responsibilities require us to apply long-range vision, the more our acts will be structured by some information developed by others rather than by personal experience. Few persons have lived such long and varied lives as to have personally experienced a great number of long-range exchanges; furthermore, many of our long-range actions are commenced comparatively early in our lives (e.g., choosing a career) before we have accrued large pools of personal experiences. These theorems lead to the following corollary:

Many important elements of our present acts are guided by our views about the acts of persons who died before we were born, and these present acts often aim to improve the status of persons who are not yet born. Such acts are an example of the Great Exchange, the remote and indirect exchange among persons who are dead, those now living, and persons yet-to-be born. These exchanges are obviously informally enforced.

The concept of the Great Exchange inevitably invites some reflection. Most human activities are influenced by both short-range and long-range considerations. Thus, parents feed their infant both because they know it will cry from hunger if the meal is postponed, and because they have some image of the conduct of that infant as an adult. But long-range considerations play a larger role in shaping our acts than we usually recognize. For instance, in the infant feeding example, the parents' vision of the future role of the matured child may rarely be articulated; but that vision undoubtedly had a large influence on most parents' decision to marry and to have a child, and thus to commit themselves to the progression of incremental episodes that leads to the infant's maturity.

In any case, a great variety of donations is made by the dependent living to the dead or unborn (and the dead and the unborn are obviously dependents), or to persons now living who will enjoy such donations long after the donor's death. All of these donations are powerfully structured by our subconscious recognition of the Great Exchange.[2] In other words, we, the independent present, make donations to either (a) the past, to repay our "debts" to them, or (b) the future, as a means of indirectly repaying our debts to the past or because we expect the future to make later donations to us. These donations are significantly related to our image of our obligation to the past; and this image will inevitably affect our opinions about the validity of our social security obligations. If we do not feel generally obligated to the past, it is unlikely that we will feel a strong responsibility to meet a heavy social security burden on behalf of people who are about to "become" the past.

Donations to the Future

Exchanges among the dead, living and unborn can first be classified by their subject matter. Thus, some of them essentially involve donations that increase the capital of persons or groups. One form of capital-increasing donation is the construction of large physical projects, when it is evident that such projects may not be finished during the lifetimes of many of the builders, or that most of their benefits will not accrue until after the death of many builders: the Cathedral of Notre Dame, which took over one hundred years to complete; the United States Capitol and the city of Washington, D.C.; and many massive dams, canals, and defense development efforts. Or, the first landing on the moon, where it was apparent that many of the "practical" benefits from that costly venture might not accrue for decades.

The implications of the long-range perspectives in such efforts are demonstrated when one contrasts the coherence of some large planned cities with the topsy-turvy nature of cities that grew without such foresight. The early days of many planned cities were frequently uncomfortable for their residents precisely because the cities were designed to be pleasing in the long-run; and so the "sacrifices," in constructing a planned city, tend to occur at the beginning for the designers, builders, and first residents. In an unplanned city, the builders and first residents have essentially opted for immediate gratification rather than sacrifice. As a result, they may pass on a disorderly environment to later cohorts. Perhaps the later cohorts may have to "straighten things out," at great cost.

There can also be long-range donations that add to a society's political capital. The American leaders who helped bring about the Revolution realized it might take many years before their effors could lead to fruition, and that during those years they might die natural deaths or even be executed. Furthermore, there were few or no significant economic benefits from revolution for most of these leaders: for example, whatever slight benefit most of them might have won through the diminishment of taxes or debts was obviously far less than the risks and frustrations they accepted through participation. But politically constructive donations can extend beyond nation-building. Many founders of institutions — colleges, religious orders, social action agencies — obviously foresaw that the major benefits resulting from their donations — if their ends were attained — would not accrue until many years had passed.

Some donations to create political and social capital can require the expenditure of human capital. Many immigrants — to America and elsewhere — were partially motivated by the aim of donating a better life to their children or other descendants. The immigrants often must have known that the benefits of immigration would not be fully realized during their lifetimes — and that their lives might even be lost in the dangers of the venture. Parents, making sacrifices to raise their children — especially in pre-industrial societies, with their short life span — are probably partly motivated by their expectation that the effects of their child-rearing will continue after their death.

Finally, in the area of capital-creating donations, we should consider the many sacrifices (both individual and collective) that are made in the pursuit of knowledge — since obviously the true significance of many intellectual discoveries is not evident until long after the discoverers and those who financed their efforts have died.

There are also donations from the living to the unborn that might be called "capital conserving." Such donations may involve the conservation of physical resources — at a cost to the present — in the interest of those still to be born. Preservation can simply mean a refusal to exploit something at the "short-range" economically optimum rate, e.g., refraining from certain forms of strip mining or lumbering, or activities that are incrementally polluting. Or it can be the economic out-of-pocket or lost opportunity costs involved in maintaining physical structures that might be of value in the future. But there can also be politically conservative acts, in which societies, or groups in societies, maintain policies or retain possession of certain rights or powers (at some cost) to assist the long-range interests of the society. (Or, conversely, we can imagine efforts to maintain "peace in our time," which may increase the likelihood of war — on highly disadvantageous terms — in our descendant's time.)

In addition to their subject matter, Great Exchanges can also be classified as tangible or intangible, and they can involve small (e.g., families) or large (e.g., societies) groups of donors.

The importance of Great Exchanges cannot be overestimated. The quality of the future is determined largely by decisions made both now and in the past. "Apres moi, le deluge," is a sure harbinger of a social tempest. And yet there are innumerable temptations for any person, institution, or society to adopt policies that maximize immediate gratification and to ignore the interests of the comparatively remote future. Indeed, one of the most remarkable social phenomena is the fact that deferred gratification — i.e., the protection of the interests of the yet-to-be born — is as pervasive as it apparently is. The reality is that, although the future has done nothing for us, much of our lives are structured by the expectation that the future *will* do something for us. This expectation leads us to the second major element of the Great Exchange: our counterdonations to the past.

Paying Our Debt to the Past

Our expectations as to how our future will assess — honor, degrade, or ignore — us are largely determined by how we go about honoring, degrading, or ignoring our own predecessors. Contributions of honor are clearly donations. In other words, suppose we regularly display conspicuous forms of gratitude because of the donations that the past (i.e., those now dead) made to us before we were born. Presumably, we will assume that the yet-to-be-born will display equivalent gratitude toward similar generosity on our part. Such reciprocal gratitude constitutes fame. Poets have long recognized fame as as a form of immortality — surely a precious good. A typical poetic expression of the aspiration for fame after death is articulated in Eliot's *Murder in the Cathedral,* where Thomas, the Archbishop of Canterbury, awaits the arrival of his murderers sent by the King. Thomas is visited by spectres, who tempt him with visions of the benefits obtainable from choosing particular options to deal with his crisis. One spectre proposes that he conduct himself so as to increase his likelihood of martyrdom and eventual glory.

> But think, Thomas, think of the glory after death.
> When king is dead, there's another king,
> And one more king is another reign.
> King is forgotten when another shall come:
> Saint and Martyr rule from the tomb.
> Think, Thomas, of enemies dismayed,
> Creeping in penance, frightened of a shade;
> Think of pilgrims, standing in line

Before the glittering jeweled shrine,
From generation to generation
Bending the knee in supplication.
Think of miracles, by God's grace,
And think of your enemies, in another place.[3]

Eliot finally portrayed a Thomas who accepted martyrdom without simultaneously desiring the fame presented by the spectre. However, it is of interest that the tempter's vision was completely fulfilled, and that Canterbury became the scene of great acts of homage by English pilgrims. Incidentally, Eliot's poem, itself, contributed to the continuation of the fame of St. Thomas Becket. In making this contribution, Eliot was undoubtedly conscious that — acting in the traditional role of the poet — he was engaged in determining our view of the past and its important figures.

Obviously, the degree of desire for fame after death possessed by different persons varies. Such variation is presumably partly the result of their socialization. Still, we can assume that persons powerfully motivated by a desire for such fame possess great emotional drive. If a society is unable to direct such drives toward important prosocial ends, it may find its fame seekers will strive toward grand and destructive goals. Such misdirected striving is also a vital literary theme.

Societies have developed an immense number of means of donating "immortal" fame to its ambitious citizens. Obviously, since death is a profoundly important event, these means serve a diversity of social and personal ends. However, as we will see, one critical goal of such donations is to give persons (and institutions — that is, collections of persons) who are now living a clue to the forms of remembrance they will receive if they model their conduct after the deceased role models now conspicuously honored.[4]

Many of these means of remembrance rely heavily on the messages transmitted by works of art: statues, paintings, poetic myths, operas, laudatory biographies. Sometimes, the names of persons are remembered through the naming of places, streets, buildings, and even nations. The coins, stamps, and documents of the society can be used to give persons fame. Institutions can be named after them. And, of course, donations of fame can be bestowed on groups of persons; thus, institutions can achieve fame through important or laudable feats that are persistently and dramatically attributed to them. Also, if histories, chronologies, or epic poems are regularly produced, contemporary prominent citizens can assume that their achievements will, in the future, be recognized in such works. Finally, many religious and ceremonial practices — masses for the dead, Memorial Day parades, Fourth of July speeches — are designed to give individual or collective recognition to the deceased, especially to those who have made significant sacrifices on behalf of the future.[5] All of these means of remembrance are usually created, maintained, and protected by various mediating agencies.

The motives that stimulate participants in these acts of remembrance vary greatly. However, the participants, who all know they will die, cannot but hope that they also will receive donations of remembrance after their own death. And, whatever their expressed motives for their actions of remembrance or recognition, the living participants perceive that those deceased persons who have made the most conspicuous positive contributions to the present society are likely to be remembered with the largest donations and for the longest periods of time. Thus, the participants who want some degree of immortality should structure their conduct so as to please those who will be living after their own death: they should be far-sighted.

We might also consider the relationship between these means of remembrance and the life of the society. The donations may be integrated into the daily life of the society: statues in parks and squares; pictures in homes; historic names, events, and ceremonies interwoven in our work, conversation, pastimes, and place names; and burial sites located near our homes. Or the society may decide that frequently contemplating the lives and achievements of the past is too costly, emotionally cumbersome, and time-consuming. To escape such demands, we may prefer to preserve the past in museums, memorialize it in remote cemeteries, or record it in scholarly books. Another aspect of the theme of remembrance is the question of whether typical citizens have a significant store of knowledge about the past of their society or even of their family. Without such knowledge, symbolic acts of remembrance lack a framework, and contemporary persons cannot conceive of their present life, itself, as being worthy of remembrance. Such knowledge, to provide an adequate framework, might include a chronology of historic events, the names of prominent dead persons, some understanding of the acts that won them prominence, an emotional appreciation of the challenges and determination that surrounded their achievements, and a recognition of the current benefits that have evolved from those achievements.[6] Many pre-industrial peoples have fully appreciated the need to transmit such historical knowledge to their descendants. One anthropologist reported the following typical anecdote about the historical orientation of the Ngoni, a central African tribe. Incidentally, note, at the close of the quote, that the report describes contemporary efforts of the Ngoni to preserve their history at the same time they are beginning to integrate their lives into modern society.

> A young man of about twenty related to me how his father, the head of a leading clan, used to talk about the Ngoni past when they went on hunting trips together on Mount Choma, where Paramount Mbelwa and His Ngoni had first settled in northern Malawi. In among the dry grass the father showed the boy the sites of former villages, the polished floors and the sturdy doorposts of the huts, and the stumps of the kraal fences. He heard in that historical setting the story of one of the famous secessions from the main Ngoni kingdom. "Early one morning," said his father, "we woke up, we who remained, and we saw that Ciwere had gone. All the people shouted 'Ciwere has separated from us. He has separated indeed. Our Paramount is poor because of his departure.' "

> It was largely through their own efforts that the Ngoni succeeded in teaching their history to their children in schools. One Ngoni minister, Reverend Y. M. Cibambo, for twenty years systematically

recorded and checked and compared Ngoni traditions. His books in the local vernacular were used
as readers in the mission schools and later
translated into English as *My Ngoni of Nyasaland.*[7]

There are aspects of remembrance other than favorable recol-
lection. Deceased persons who are seen as conspicuously reprehensible
in the judgment of later generations have attained immortal infamy;
Judas Iscariot, Guy Fawkes, Benedict Arnold. (By remembering to
despise such persons, we honor those who rejected temptation.)
Sometimes, too, particular factions in wars or social conflicts
realize that, if they lose, they will be remembered largely from the
perspective of the winners and their descendants. Such a possibility
presents the threat of permanent collective obliquy; this was the
fate of the American Loyalists after the Revolution, and the Southern
slaveholders after the Civil War. A society or social class may become
extinct because of drastic social change, and the persons who continue to inhabit their land will not donate remembrance to these
predecessors. Fear of such infamy or obliquy may stimulate groups
and individuals to avoid conduct that might provoke such disas-
trous effects.

The Economy of Remembrance

There is inevitably an "economy" that governs our remembrance of the dead. Thus, it is correct to call remembrance a
"donation." Conspicuous remembrance requires time and material
resources to present artistic works, conduct ceremonies, or create
symbols; and even the number of streets, places, and structures
that can receive memoralizing names if finite. (And when we give
persons' names to streets — as compared to numbers, like East
53rd Street — we also complicate our problems in finding street
locations.) But the number of dead persons is immense. To
protect us from being overwhelmed with obligations to the past,
a priority of remembrance is maintained. The nature of this
system is easily recognizable. We are more likely to remember
(make donations to) recently deceased persons, or prominent

persons who died in the more remote past. This system means we are steadily going through a process of "forgetting" the dead, and their contributions, and of simultaneously adding newly deceased persons to our pool of donees. But the word "prominence" does not have a continuously stable application. It is dynamic because the lives of many significant deceased humans (or long-lived institutions) were complex, and different persons may make different judgments about such complex lives, or make those judgments from new information that may be discovered about them. Thus, the comparative prominence of deceased persons changes, as well as the donations directed toward honoring achievements.

Different persons or mediating institutions will also desire to use our visions of the past for different purposes. As a result, they will selectively screen and present information about currently prominent dead persons to advance their aspirations. Or, opinion-formers may aggressively pursue and publicize derogatory information about such persons. For example, our opinions about the meaning of the world today are partly affected by our views of our past: suppose Washington was a closet homosexual? suppose Robert E. Lee embezzeled large amounts of money from the Confederate government while his soldiers were starving? suppose Mussolini had engaged in effective covert activities to save many Italian Jews? and so on. Such "discoveries" — or arguable interpretations — might not only affect our views of the persons involved, but also have reverberations that might affect peoples' views about contemporary issues. Thus, the process of distributing and redistributing honors to the dead is not neutral. Finally, changing contemporary circumstances may cause a reconsideration of the value to be attached to past leaders and their "achievements," or there may arise a desire to discover and elevate "forgotten" heroes whose modes of real or imagined conduct we wish to see presently emulated.

But there is more to making donations to the past than deciding priorities among competing deceased leaders or organizations, or even deciding the view to be adopted towards their conduct. There is also the question of how much of a society's resources should be dedicated to such donations. Mediating institutions may persuade us to dedicate high proportions of resources to paying reverence to the achievements of the dead. Such memorialization draws resources away from other activities and encourages continuation of the forms of conduct that have earned such praise.[8] It may not be exact to say that this pattern will automatically lead to social stability; the conduct encouraged may be, in some sense, destabilizing, e.g., warfare or geographical explorations. However, dedicating a great deal of resources to paying reverence to the past clearly creates certain benefits for a society. For instance, most persons who have attained posthumous fame displayed great fortitude and foresight during their lives, i.e., they practiced conspicuous delayed gratification. Reverence for leaders of the past stimulates the continuation of that conduct in present cohorts.

Acts of reverence for the past probably also provide gratification for living persons, who can assume — in their day-to-day life — that, after their death, they may attain similar immortality. On the other hand, some honored deceased leaders may have engaged in forms of conduct that are no longer socially adaptive; they may no longer be appropriate role models. Still, in assessing previous leaders and the "deficiencies" in their conduct, we must distinguish between the time-bound elements of their conduct (e.g., Jefferson, like almost all prosperous Southerners of his period, was a slaveholder), and those elements that have persisting value (e.g., Jefferson was broadly learned and dedicated his life to public causes).

We can also have societies that do not apply substantial resources to honoring the past. This "degradation" of the past frees such societies from the obligation to make elaborate donations to the past and releases resources for other activities. In societies freed from the weight of the past, and the encumbrances of mediating institutions, citizens will tend to govern their conduct by the tests of immediate and intermediate gratification. Perhaps this is what is meant by the pursuit of happiness. These tests can provide people with a degree of flexibility that can often be productive. While it may not always be wise to pursue policies that generate bad immediate outcomes in the hope that they will eventually be productive, it is true that many policies with productive outcomes faced great obstacles in their early stages. In sum, it is not always easy to determine when the pursuit of speedy gratification — by either people or institutions — represents adaptability or faddishness. Of course, if a society that does not make donations to honor the past "needs" to enlist its citizens in long-range endeavors, it may well encounter serious motivation problems.

Another difficulty generated by comparative ignorance of the past arises from the fact that most living adults are inevitably concerned about the nature of their remembrance after death (i.e., their immortality), especially if the society has moved above the level of bare subsistence. These aspirations for remembrance can be mobilized by fame-seeking leaders who help citizens attain immortality by provoking them to accomplish dangerous, memorable feats. Essentially, the plea of such leaders to the followers is: act as I propose and you will be remembered. These leaders create new mediating institutions or drastically revise old ones. If there are not popular role models (of honored, historic persons) suggesting the forms of conduct that deserve immortality, the oblivion-fleeing leaders will invent their own definitions of fame. They may even argue that "horrible" conduct will surely be remembered, and that it is possible — given the unstable existing remembrance system — that the future may judge to be noble an act now deemed horrible. This precise argument was proffered by some of the Nazi leaders to explain the Holocaust. After all, one of the prime agitational techniques of the Nazis was to reshape the existing German vision of their past. It is well-known that the Nazi leaders had a special affinity for the music of Wagner, who portrayed a remote and terror-ridden past in heroic and powerful art.

Managing our Evaluation of the Past

The discussion of our shifting opinions about the dead suggests that these views are shaped by institutions or persons who are deliberately concerned with affecting those opinions. And, of course, any continuing society must include entities with such "management" responsibilities. These entities mediate exchanges among the past, present, and future. At one extreme, the mediators can be as conscious and overt as the agency portrayed in Orwell's novel *1984*, where a protagonist was employed in regularly rewriting history (and obliterating previous history) to meet changing priorities in a hypothetical totalitarian society. At the other extreme, mediators can be as pervasive and informal as storytellers and bards, who orally recite tales of heroic tradition to their young and old listeners. Between these two extremes, we can recognize a variety of mediating entities: religious organizations; veterans groups; governmental institutions, ranging from the post office (making decisions about stamps) to fine arts commissions; educational institutions; the media; and diverse private organizations. There are also various categories of individuals who perceive that appeals to "the noble traditions of the past" are useful for generating certain forms of future-oriented actions, or that the reconstructions of the past can serve political ends. The effectiveness of these individuals is determined by some combination of their creative ability and the immediate demands facing society. In any case, leaders of many powerful causes have found that presenting an integrated poetic image of the past, present, and future is a potent device for mobilizing people behind difficult enterprises.

Many of the themes just treated, dealing with managing and using the past, and relating past, present, and future, are vividly illustrated in the famous funeral oration of Pericles, as described by Thucydides. The oration was delivered in about 420 B. C., to commemorate the first Athenian dead of the Peloponnesian War. Thucydides first described the careful preparation of the remains of the deceased and the ceremonies which preceded the placing of their bones in a sepulchere. Then Pericles, "a man chosen by the state, of approved wisdom and eminent reputation" prepared to pronounce over them an "appropriate panegyric." Pericles said:

> I shall begin with our ancestors: it is both just and proper that they should have the honor of first mention on an occasion like the present. They dwelt in this country without break in the succession from generation to generation, and handed it down free to the present time by their valour. And if our more remote ancestors deserve praise, much more do our own fathers, who added to their inheritance the empire we now possess.... But what was the road by which we reached our position, what the form of government under which our greatness grew, what the national habits out of which it sprang; these are questions which I try to solve before I proceed to my panegyric....

My panegyric is now in great measure complete;
for the Athens I have celebrated is only what
the heroism of these and men like them have
made her, men whose fame, unlike that of most
Hellenes, will be found to be only commensurate
with their desserts. And if a test of worth be
wanted, it is to be found in their closing scene, and
this not only in the cases in which it set
the final seal upon their merit, but also in those in
which it gave the first intimation of their having
any. For there is justice in the claim that steadfast-
ness in his country's battles should be as a cloak
to cover a man's other imperfections, since the
good action has blotted out the bad, and his
merit as a citizen more than outweighed his de-
merits as an individual. But none of these allowed
either wealth with its prospect of future enjoyment
to unnerve his spirit, or poverty with its hope of a
day of freedom and riches to tempt him to shirk
from danger....

So died these men as became Athenians. You,
their survivors, must determine to have as unalter-
ing resolution in the field, though you may pray
that it may have a happier issue....you must
yourselves realize the power of Athens, and feed
your eyes upon her from day to day, till love
of her fills your hearts; and then when all her
greatness shall break upon you, you must reflect
that it was by courage, sense of duty and a keen
feeling of honour in action that men were enabled
to win all this, and that no personal failure in
an enterprise could make them consent to deprive
their country of valour, but they laid it at her
feet as the most glorious contribution they could
make. For this offering of their lives made in
common by them all they each of them individually

received that renown which never grows old.... For
heroes have the whole earth as their tomb....[9]

Thucydides noted that throughout the war, a similar custom
was observed at all of the burials. We can easily see how the
speech meshes with our model of the Great Exchange. Pericles,
a great orator and sympathetic to the cause for which the heroes
died, was selected by "the state" to deliver their panegyric. In
other words, talent, always a scarce resource, was assigned to
facilitate remembrance. The oration was preceded by elaborate ceremonies. It opened with praise of the Athenians' more remote
ancestors and gradually approached the situation of the present
cohorts. The central portion of the speech was an eloquent analysis
and tribute to Athenian customs and institutions. Pericles then directly
praised the persons being interred. He mentioned that courage on
behalf of the society may excuse a variety of personal faults. He
called on the listeners to observe the noble city that surrounded
them, to be filled with love for it, and, if necessary, to emulate the
immortal heroes being commemorated. In exchange for such courage,
the listeners were implicitly promised a panegyric of equivalent grandeur.
Finally, Thucydides, a profound thinker and writer, chose to "donate"
effort to portray the whole episode in an ennobling perspective.

We should also recognize that the economy of honoring the dead
is related to the size of the mediating institutions involved. Larger
institutions can create more "fame" since the pool of rememberers
and the resources available for constructing symbolic works of art
are enlarged. However, such institutions are also less able to give
individual remembrance to high proportions of their deceased individual members: it would simply take too much of the time of the living
citizens. Conversely, while small institutions (e.g., families) can provide
less massive remembrance, their limited size also means that they can
afford to give individual recognition to each (comparatively recently)
deceased member. Of course, smaller institutions, in making their
"decisions" about individual acts of remembrance will be influenced
by the customs prevailing throughout the society (e.g., the patterns
of mourning), and the forms of family-type remembrance supported
by various institutions that relate to the families of deceased persons.

This outline of family and extra-family remembrance suggests a concentric pattern of systems for honoring the dead. Small institutions, such as the family, give serious individual attention to all deserving members, while larger entities individually recognize only the prominent deceased and give collective recognition to groups of deceased persons who have made significant contributions. Of course, the outline implies that a society wishing to stimulate far-sighted conduct among the participants in its small and large institutions must have a medley of means of demonstrating to the living that deserving persons will be remembered (in different ways) by various social institutions after their death. Indeed, an institution that cannot make donations to its more loyal members after their death is an institution that will have difficulty stimulating long-range loyalty. We can also see that each form or act of conspicuous remembrance by an institution reinforces other institutions within the same social system to engage in their appropriate counterpart acts.

Our Debts to Our Parents

At this point, we should make particular reference to the relationship between living and dead (or younger and older) family members. Living descendants can both *honor* their dead parents by burial and mourning rites, and *bring honor* to them by their day-to-day conduct. We have already implicitly touched on the nature of the social forces that sustain patterns of mourning and burial rites. Obviously, conspicuously successful children (who "succeed" either as children or adults) bring pride to their living parents and "honor" to their dead ones. In many geographically stable societies, a person's success in adult public life was a reflection on his parents' competency: in small, pre-industrial English villages, "Yeoman Johnson" was recognized as the "son of John"; everyone knew John and was interested in having the tie between John and his son kept in the foreground. Under these circumstances, what happened to "Johnson" reflected — for better or worse — on John. There have been other patterns of symbolic in-family remembrance: family estates, businesses, coats of arms, and traditions of conduct.[10] When parents live in environments where their children's conduct can bring them significant pride or disgrace, they are prone to rear children trained to make the appropriate donations, i.e., to act so the parents gain honor. When child-rearing gets difficult — as it sometimes must — the parents are prepared to meet and conquer such stress, in order to inculcate appropriate traits in their descendants. Of course, these traits may also cause their descendants to be more effective citizens in general.

It should not be surprising that children have mixed feelings about this responsibility to donate to their parents by honoring them and bringing them honor. The responsibility may compel them to undertake uncomfortable or dangerous actions.[11] On the other hand, if a child "rejects" this responsibility proffered by his parents, he breaks the chain of responsibility with past generations (and here "generations" is the proper word). In the future, he will have difficulty demanding or attaining equivalent satisfaction from his own children. At the least, (and this proposition should have special significance in a society that has invented the concept of the identity crisis), the requirement of bringing honor to one's parents provides a ready source of identity.

The quality of in-family socialization of children to the Great Exchange is affected by actuarial patterns. In particular, the longer the average adult life span in a society, the more remote death will seem to children or to the parents of young children. In our era, death is chronologically remote from most young persons. Thus, young parents may be unconscious of the formal, symbolic deference they will hope to attain — directly and indirectly — after death; they have not thought deeply enough about death to realize what constitutes "immortality." As a result, such parents may fail to socialize their children to the Great Exchange, and the children — also lacking contact with death — may not realize what is "expected" of them. By the time the parents have become older and wiser, their children are, for practical purposes, beyond their control.

The Discipline of History

This outline has not yet considered a peculiarly contemporary form of mediating agency: the modern academic discipline of history. To many lay persons, this discipline is dedicated to discovering the objective truth about the past, just as we might hope to discover the "truth" about cancer or weather forecasting. And, to some degree, the discipline does have some members who pursue and disseminate knowledge about the dead with the same objectivity as researchers generally do the physical sciences. However, the attainment of such objectivity is not the central social effect of the discipline.

The amount of information attainable about the past is vast, and true "objectivity" requires the searcher either to focus on a relatively limited subject area or to produce exhaustive, elaborate studies. Neither approach serves to offer the average intelligent citizen much inspirational information about the past — which has been a prime motive for human concerns with history. Furthermore, a significant proportion of our contemporaries who write history are inevitably influenced by a (natural) desire to affect public attitudes about the dead. Without this motivation, how many persons would bother to pursue such a highly arduous career? And so many historians — whether they are academics or popularizers — behind their formal shield of objectivity, are striving to change the present public attitudes about society by changing our understanding of the life of persons now dead.[12] This is inevitable, and thus "natural." But the problem is that many of these managers of our past are less "accountable" to the polity than were the primitive story tellers who recited the Odyssey in Greek marketplaces, or medieval chroniclers, or Shakespeare and his troupe when they presented the history plays.

The storytellers, religious leaders, and politicians who previously helped to manage the past — and thus to mediate between the living and the dead — were overtly dependent upon public contributions or votes for their survival. Without such popular "consent," their power to reshape the past would have expired. Because of this pressure, their donations tended to support traditional values. In contrast, contemporary academic historians are often only remotely connected to the taxpayers and trustees who pay for their work. Therefore, they feel little pressure to adopt protective attitudes toward popular views of the past. Their allegedly dispassionate, technical approaches provide them with shields against criticism and protect them from demands that they promote images of the dead that are useful to the majority of the society. The problems of contemporary academic historians (and history teachers) are further compounded by the discrepancy between the original aspirations that many of them have had — to assume a bard-like, semi-poetic mediating role — and the specialized, constraining nature of much of their work. This discrepancy must engender a good deal of frustration in some historians. That frustration may spill over into hostility toward their society and some of its traditions, which they are expected to protect.

It might now be wise to summarize some of the main theses that have come to light in our analysis of the Great Exchange.

A Restatement

Words like "the past" or "history" simply describe the means we use to characterize the conduct of persons who are usually now dead. Individuals, institutions, and societies give great weight to their appreciation of the past in planning and carrying out their long-range plans. They understand that their own conduct may continue to have its effects in the remote future, and that, in that future, they will be assessed by persons and institutions alive after their own death. Thus, contemporary "actors," in striving to anticipate these remote responses to their conduct, base their forecasts on the assessments of the past now being made about them — and in which they participate.

These assessments of the past can range from praise and honor to indifference, and finally to hostility and debasement. Different elements of some particular period in the past can be weighted in different ways. The assessments that are made of some past period can vary among different cohorts alive at the same time, or among different social classes, and will probably vary during different eras.

The assessments of the past made by individuals are largely the result of their own socialization. In other words, the society, with its innumerable mediating institutions, "teaches" its successive cohorts how they should feel about the past. Such lessons proffered by any large society can never be completely coherent, because of the complexity of the problem, and the many divergent sources of knowledge around the children and adolescents being socialized. Still, some general principles of effective socialization to the Great Exchange can be inferred. A great deal of material and social resources should be donated to the task: the time of many persons in different cohorts; the talents and goods to create works of art; the economic cost of conserving symbols honoring historic achievements; and the dedication of social forces to protect famous persons of the past from symbolic degradation. In particular, the society must have some generally coherent and favorable image of its past and understand the value of such an image for advancing the future welfare of the society. Where a change in the existing assessment of the past is necessary, the mediating agencies "managing" that change must imaginatively strive to merge the needs of adaptation and preservation.

Not all societies continue to honor the once great feats of their past. Some societies may decide they are confronted with a radically different situation than existed in their past, and choose to degrade their former heroes. They then find others from the past or create a new class of contemporary heroes. But this restructuring implies the existence of an interregnum. During this interregnum, the past is degraded and substitute heroes are created. A disturbing instability may exist during this time as some mediating agencies struggle to preserve "the past," and others strive to compel acceptance of the new heroes and the changed patterns of conduct that come with such acceptance. Furthermore, the new contemporary heroes, who are being "created," can only win continuing fame through dramatic heroic acts. Such achievements often occur during bloody, dramatic conflicts. All in all, the effective degradation of the past and the creation of a new cosmogony is not a pretty thing to contemplate. There are also societies that decide to ignore their past (i.e., not to be concerned about the Great Exchange) because they believe the past is irrelevant. Implicitly, they are determining that all life must be shaped by actions that transpire completely within the lifetime of the participants. This principle might apply for some primitive, nomadic tribes of hunters and gatherers. Such tribes may plant nothing, "possess" no territory, and have only a low capability for injuring their environment. Still, they expect their children speedily to assume responsibilities (perhaps by the age of eight, their children are equalling the production of adults in many activities).

It is clearly impossible for any modern society to ignore the past and survive very long. Modern societies that try to ignore their past will discover they face great difficulties in shaping large projects, conserving resources, making long-range plans, or socializing their young to practice deferred gratification as adults. Policies will become increasingly erratic, unprincipled, and unsound. Personal relations will

be pervaded with equivalent instability. Ultimately, this instability —
and lack of sense of permanence — will become intolerable. Then, the
citizens of this society will begin to seek clues from its past — or
from someone's past — as to how to attain immortality. Sellers of
the past — or of alternative pasts — will arise. These salesmen will
necessarily be charismatic; they can be either good or evil. Eventually,
a "purchase" will be made. And the pursuit of immortality, through
one means or another, will begin again.

...if the several States, many of which have already laid the foundation of munificent establishments of local beneficence...shall be led to suppose, as they will be, should this bill become a law, that Congress is to make provision for such objects, the fountains of charity will be dried up at home, and the several States, instead of bestowing their own means on the social wants of their own people, may themselves, through the strong temptation, which appeals to States as well as individuals, become humble supplicants for the bounty of the Federal Government, reversing their true relation to this Union.

—**President Franklin Pierce**, his veto message regarding a bill to provide federal aid to finance mental institutions, 1848[1]

CHAPTER 4

Helping Dependent Persons in Industrial Society

We have seen that pre-industrial societies had elaborate, and often rather effective means of providing help to dependent persons. Gradually, these means were transformed into many of the practices that prevail in our era. The transformation was very incremental, and affected by a variety of forces. An understanding of the general nature of this transformation will help us to understand where we are at this time. And so this chapter portrays the evolution of exchanges among independent and dependent persons and groups in the United States and Great Britain, from the period preceding the passage of the Elizabethan Poor Law of 1601 to the Great Depression of the 1930's. The material gives special attention to exchanges among age groups. In particular, it will identify themes that are pertinent to issues still vital in our time.

Many shifts occurred in the nature of these exchanges through this period. These shifts were subjected to searching and thoughtful contemporary debates. A number of these debates clearly anticipated problems facing our current reciprocity systems. And the quality of

intellectual articulation on these earlier occasions undoubtedly benefit-
ed from the existence of certain mediating groups that today are muted,
and from the comparative absence of some others. In other words,
earlier writers did not aim to produce textbooks to be sold to students
in schools of social work or education, and public leaders could make
direct but thoughtful formal statements that today would expose them
to dramatic political repercussions.

While the presentation will focus on intercohort transactions, it
will frequently cover policies affecting donations of poor or needy
persons in general, since the forces shaping these latter practices often
simultaneously affected intercohort donations. Pertinent developments
in Great Britain and America through this era did not always run
parallel. Still, during most of the era, patterns of British policy were
the major external influence in shaping American policy in exchanges
among independent and dependent groups.

There were, of course, certain trends whose history is extraneous
to the present work, but whose incremental development during the era
inevitably shaped the changing patterns of reciprocity. Let me simply
list these developments, without explicitly discussing their implications.
Those implications will become evident as the discussion proceeds.

The beginning of the era closely coincided with the commencement
of the Protestant Reformation. Means of transportation steadily im-
proved throughout the period, both increasing human mobility and
helping to stimulate trade. The development of the printing press
assisted the spread and growth of knowledge. Literacy increased. More
and more exchanges were based on money, and so the market economy
spread. The development of double-entry bookkeeping, and other
sophisticated systems of accounting, encouraged the growth of larger,
and the reduction of family-based, businesses. Urbanization increased,
and the proportion of the rural population concomitantly declined.
Occupations became more specialized. Industrialization grew. The
general level of affluence increased. And national governments grew
in authority.

The Poor Law: Formalized Enforcement

During the sixteenth century, a number of developments in England
put particular stress on the existing immediate tangible patterns of in-

tercohort reciprocity, and generally on the means of providing sustenance for dependent persons.[2] For instance, the Reformation closed monasteries and other traditional church-based mediating systems for assisting citizens to help the poor. The Black Plague left many children orphans. The Plague also caused a shortage of farm labor in many areas. This shortage caused peasants to leave their traditional communities and travel in pursuit of better employment. Such mobility was an unusual phenomenon, and the travelers, who had no money, usually begged to earn their keep while on the road. (Of course, there had been travelers in earlier periods, but they had come from the upper-classes, and were identified as such by their dress, speech, and manners. These upper-class travelers were "entitled" to hospitality (i.e., a donation) at the homes of other members of their class, even though the hosts and guests were not personally acquainted. Both hosts and guests had been socialized to the principles of indirect informal reciprocity accepted by their class; in effect, the guests understood that they, at their own homes, would be obliged to donate similar hospitality to other travelers.) Finally, the English cloth trade grew, and the cloth makers essentially supported themselves in a market economy.

These developments were highly disruptive to English society. Mobile poor persons were released, by their transiency, from many of the existing constraints against crime, since most criminal laws were enforced in communities of ten to twenty miles in diameter. A person who traveled left his accusers behind him, and was thus freed from many deterrents. Again, the high number of orphaned children and young persons taxed the informal reciprocity systems of small rural villages; indeed, such youths often joined, or were recruited into, roving bands of beggars.[3] And unemployed industrial workers had neither manor lords nor crops from their farms to turn to for sustenance in hard times.

In over one hundred years, a succession of national laws in England were passed which attempted to stabilize the situation. The Elizabethan Poor Law, passed in 1601, was essentially a codification of the preceding statutes. In discussing the Poor Law, it is thus justifiable to include, without specification, provisions which were technically promulgated in earlier Parliamentary statutes during the sixteenth century. The Law attempted to articulate a number of prevailing implicit principles relating to reciprocity among independent and dependent groups, and then to formalize and apply those principles to the immediate situation. The Law included a recital of the problems that confronted the society. "All parts of this realm of England and Wales be presently with rogues, vagabonds and sturdy beggars exceedingly pestered, by means whereof daily happeneth in the same realm horrible murders, thefts, and other great outrages...And forasmuch as charity would that poor, aged, and impotent persons should as necessarily be provided for as the said rogues, vagabonds, and sturdy beggars repressed...."[4] The Law then prescribed measures in response to the challenge:

1. No poor person (i.e., someone without visible means of support) could live in any parish but that of his birth. This was called the principle of "settlement." The provision aimed to subject each poor person — whom the society deemed especially prone to commit unlawful acts — to the persistent scrutiny of his own local community. Any poor person found outside his parish would be punished and returned to his parish.

2.   Each parish of the Church of England was designated as the mediating system for maintaining the poor persons born in its confines. The responsibility was to be met by levying necessary taxes in each parish. The parish tax rate was determined by its proportion of poor persons. Parish overseers of the poor, elected by the parishioners, were responsible for the maintenance of the system. Local Justices of the Peace, whose jurisdiction included a number of parishes, were designated to insure these parish obligations were met, and to hear complaints from allegedly aggrieved poor persons. In 1601, there were approximately 16,000 parishes in England, so the parish was an extremely small administrative unit. Obviously, the assumption was that the concentration of responsibility for donations in such units would provoke independent community members to socialize their potentially dependent neighbors to reciprocity and responsible citizenship.

3.   Poor persons were entitled to beg in the confines of their parish, since the law did not intend to relieve independent citizens of their Christian duty to decide to donate alms. Various enactments, both before and after the Poor Law, required communities to license or otherwise publicly designate authorized beggars, to insure that citizens would be importuned only by "deserving" persons.

4. The parents, grandparents, and children of poor persons seeking support from their parish were legally obligated to contribute to their maintenance.

5. Adjudicated poor persons, who were entitled to donations from their parishes, were required to do work for the parish (as a counterdonation), typically in a parish workhouse. Usually, such a workhouse was associated with a poorhouse, a residence for poor persons, which was also provided and managed by the parish.

The Poor Law was clearly grounded on many traditional elements of informal reciprocity. Its goals inextricably combined the two aims of the protection of the independent, competent, and healthy, and the provision of the welfare of dependent members of society. It assumed that communities should assist their needy members. It aimed to maintain proximate networks of donation within the family and the parish. It established a system for determining who was deserving. It recognized that formal enforcement was only a stop-gap recourse, and gave first priority to maintaining and strengthening existing systems of informal enforcement. And it tried to establish structures that encouraged donees to proffer counterdonations, which made donees conscious of their obligated status. The Law was a departure from the past in that it included a formal enforcement structure (a) which governed both donors (they were taxed) and donees and their relatives, and (b) under which entitlements and obligations were determined by an official.

Other Systems for Informal Enforcement

Inevitably, the Law was only one of several incremental innovations tried by the Elizabethans to deal with the challenge before them. Another measure was the Statute of Trusts, passed in 1597, which created new means for wealthy persons to make donations for dependent persons or to establish persisting charitable trusts. W. K. Jordan, the most thorough student of this development, concluded that the amount of wealth donated to social purposes in England for many decades after the passage of the Poor Law — as a result of the "movement" symbolized by the Statute of Trusts — greatly surpassed the funds taxed and distributed through the operation of the Poor Law.[5] Essentially, a great deal of the new wealth created by merchants, manufacturers, and landowners in the dynamic society was gradually donated to support the establishment of schools, hospitals, retirement homes, and a variety of other charitable purposes. Indeed, many of the utilities that are typically maintained at taxpayers' expense in our time — bridges, highways — were often built and sustained by such "voluntary" donations, just as in the time of Classic Greece. (Incidentally, the increase in these secular donations was concurrent with a dramatic decrease in donations for formally religious purposes.)

Of course, the legal structure established by the Statute of Trusts was only one element assisting this dramatic flow of donations. A vast medley of symbolic, religious, nationalistic, and poetic devices provided the emotional stimulus which informally enforced the donations. For instance, the various Protestant groups that formed in England after the Reformation tended to view effective entreprenuerism as a sign of God's grace, and thus they encouraged the growth of entrepreneurial attitudes. Simultaneously, many ministers — through both their sermons and writings — stressed the obligation of successful persons to view their wealth as a stewardship from God, and to apply it to pro-social ends.

A typical religious pamphlet, *Three Sermons to Movue Compassion Towards the Poor*, stated that: "the rich man is no more than God's steward, and the poor man's treasurer...give your money...and you shall have God's treasures...rewards in this life and the world to come."[6] Another powerful device for enforcing donations from the affluent was the funeral sermon. On such occasions, the friends and relatives of the dead person collected to hear a minister deliver an extended sermon analyzing the deceased's life and work. Often, these sermons were published and distributed. Prominent citizens must have attended many such ceremonies during their lives. Inevitably, these occasions must have stimulated them to consider what remarks would be made and circulated about them after their own deaths. Typically, such sermons carefully assessed the generosity of the deceased, and dramatically warned listeners of the dire consequences of a selfish life. One preacher, in a funeral sermon titled *A Patterne for All*, delivered in 1658, observed that "greatness without goodnesse will be but as a great fagot to burne more in hell." The preacher went on to observe that the deceased was the soul of charities because "the poore round him, his heart, his hand, and his gate was ever open to them, the widow, the fatherless, the lame, the impotent, the poore children of the neighbour parishes were relieved constantly at his gates....he hath dispersed and given to the poore, his rightousness endureth...."[7] As one example of the effects of this process, between 1480 and 1660, over four hundred endowed grammar schools were founded in England as a result of private donations ("endowment" meant that the founder left a trust fund which would pay for all or part of the continuing costs of the school).[8] Naturally, such schools developed numerous means of remembering the creator's generosity: founder's day ceremonies, appropriately named buildings, memorial portraits, and other devices.

Adapting to the New World

In the New World, the challenges confronting the English settlers provided occasions for reiteration of patterns of reciprocity developed in their homeland. Most of the colonies adopted legislation akin to the English Poor Law. Such legislation continued the principle of settlement; that is, it required poor persons who wanted donations to demonstrate they were residents of the area before they applied for relief. Furthermore, the laws made parents and children liable for assisting each other, provided for the establishment of local poorhouses and workhouses, and typically, made the counties the basic units of administration and taxation for the purpose of supporting "their own" paupers.[9] However, the adoption of measures patterned on the Poor Law could only partially resolve the reciprocity demands stimulated by life in colonial America. On the one hand, a high level of interdependence was essential among persons who hoped to survive in a wilderness environment, where unforeseeable emergencies required citizens to look routinely to one another for aid. For instance, the text of a sermon delivered at sea in 1630 to English Puritans who had embarked from Massachusetts urged that, for the colonists to succeed, and

> to provide for our posterity...we must be knit together in this work as one man, we must entertain one another in brotherly affection, we must be

> willing to abridge ourselves of our superfluities
> for the supply of others' necessities, we must up-
> hold a commerce together in all meekness, gentle-
> ness, patience and liability, we must delight in each
> other, make others' conditions our own, rejoice
> together, mourn together, labor and suffer together,
> always having before our eyes our commission and
> community in the work...if we acquit ourselves
> well the Lord shall make us a praise and glory,
> that men may say of succeeding plantations, the
> Lord make it like that of New England. For we
> must consider that we shall be as a city upon a hill,
> that the eyes of all people are upon us. So that if
> we deal falsely with our God in this work we have
> undertaken...we shall be made a story and a by-
> word throughout the World.[10]

On the other hand, despite such profound and appropriate aspirations, some environmental characteristics of the New World tended to
frustrate these pro-reciprocity aims. Many traditional English social
institutions that mediated reciprocal conduct could not easily be easily
transplanted and/or sustained in frontier America. Furthermore, the
successful exploitation of a frontier environment required entrepreneurial
and individualistic attitudes that conflicted with the concurrent need
for persisting reciprocity. Consequently, the colonists began to fear
that their traditional culture — and, indeed, prospects for any continuing humane society — might be submerged as their descendents
matured with values more akin to the savages than to their parents.[11]
To deal with this terrible challenge, the settlers placed increasing
reliance on schools as a critical device for socializing their children
to adult life — which meant socializing them to practice reciprocity.
And so legislation was passed requiring local communities to maintain
schools out of their tax money, and to encourage children to attend
such schools. In effect, the colonists hoped that the schools would
substitute for the Old World socializing patterns maintained by
churches, community stability, and apprenticeship. For instance, the
New England Primer, used in American schools in the early eighteenth

century, taught reading lessons through materials which persistently urged children to parental obedience, and emphasized the grievous punishments which might be visited on disobedient children during life and after their death.[12]

The diverse tensions surrounding the application of reciprocity in early New England arose from elements endemic to frontier life: the need for cooperation; the temptations and practical requirements encouraging independence (which might expand into selfishness); and the persisting need to develop and maintain deliberate socializing institutions. These tensions persisted throughout the succeeding centuries of American immigration, exploration, and settlement. Thus, in 1839, a settler in Michigan observed that borrowing was so common on the frontier that owners of useful property — wheelbarrows, shovels, saddles — expected such equipment to spend half its useful life in the possession of neighbors.[13] Again, an American book of practical advice for prairie settlers, published in 1861, advised members of companies of traveling settlers to sign a compact, obligating each family to contribute to a common fund, to compensate families whose animals or wagons might give out.[14] But developing concurrently with these pro-cooperation attitudes was the image of the independent pioneer, trapper, cowboy, miner, or entrepreneur.

A uniquely American schizophrenia gradually evolved: popular values gave great weight simultaneously to dramatic (almost anti-social) independence, and to the concept of teamwork (which represents cooperation). Indeed, Americans were the first society to use the word "teamwork" to describe a group of athletes cooperating together. That semantic invention is consonant with American fascination with the theme of persons choosing to bind themselves under formal rules to work to a common end. Examples of this tendency can be recognized in the Mayflower Compact, the United States Constitution, and even in the instructions to the prairie settlers mentioned above. In one sense, these various deliberate communities were "voluntary." The members chose to form them. However, powerful environmental forces often constrained the parameters of such choices, e.g., the settlers in the Mayflower knew that if they did not negotiate a compact before landing, they would either face the wilderness as a dis-integrated group, or turn their ship around and sail back to England. In any event, cooperation — in contrast to independence — was probably the predominant American value; at the same time, independence represented a more prominent norm in America than in most societies.

School as a Means to Foster Reciprocity

To insure that the children raised in the unstable frontier environment were socialized to reciprocity, the settlers' churches, social welfare and governmental agencies all gave great prominence to school as a socializing institution.

The schools were given even enlarged prominence as continuing streams of immigrants flowed into the country, especially as those immigrants came from societies with linguistic and/or cultural traditions that diverged from those of the dominant American social classes. Unless such divergencies were moderated, the native-born Americans feared it might be difficult for widespread reciprocity to be practiced — there would simply not be an adequate body of common, binding understandings. And so schools were given an important mediating role in socializing the children of these immigrants to reciprocity as practiced in America. Some historical revisionists have contended that the significance of schools in this activity has been considerably overemphasized.[15] Of course, quantitative evaluation of their role is difficult. Still, as a practical matter, it is hard to envision how an industrial society would carry out such a socializing process without appropriately giving great weight to its schools: in industrial society, the school was the major non-family agency in touch with the child from (let us say) the ages of 6 to 12. Without such an agency, the child would tend to spend these years surrounded almost entirely by his parents' "foreign" language and values. If the society has determined to socialize certain values in that child (beyond those of his parents), it would obviously be desirable to begin such socialization before the child attained the age of 12. The institution handling that socialization would appropriately be a school.

Formally enforced public taxes played a larger role in supporting early American schools than they did in England. Still, private, informally enforced donations to assist public education were still quite significant.

For example, in New York City, up until 1830, elementary schools for children from poor families were maintained by the Public School Society, a private organization. While the Society received a state subsidy, each year the Society's 50 to 100 uncompensated trustees made up to 100,000 inspection visits to its schools.[16] And De Witt Clinton, a two term governor of the state served for many years as President of the Society. Colleges were largely dependent on private donations and tuition. As a result, nearly all American colleges operating before the Civil War were supported by the donations of members of religious denominations.

Of course, as in the case of many donations to help children and youths, charges have been levelled that the donors who encouraged the spread of formal education were "essentially" motivated by selfish personal interests — to "keep down" the lower classes and provide more tractable labor. Such charges err in attributing simple motives to acts based on enormously complex considerations. To put it quite concretely, any adult who has ever made a decision to marry (or get divorced), pursue a particular career, or buy a home at some particular location, realizes that such individual personal decisions are usually the outcome of an enormous variety of "causes." Most people would call someone naive who tended to attribute any such decisions to one central reason. Similarly, common sense and personal experience suggest that most individuals who make donations to assist the young are motivated by an equivalent variety of causes. Explanations that principally focus on single causes tell us as much about the "explainers" as about the phenomenon they attempt to analyze. After all, if the allegedly "altruistic" donors are largely selfish and manipulative, why should we not imagine that the allegedly "objective" explainers are equally deceptive and unreliable? In either case, we are entitled to base our conclusions about the motives of people in the past partly on our contemporary experience, and partly on our observations of the people we see about us, serving as PTA officers, volunteer tutors, scout troop leaders, and so on. Do we perceive these adults as essentially motivated by a desire to keep the young (or lower classes) in their place? And if we reject this proposition, why should we assume that comparative virtue exists only in our era?

Deficiencies in Poor Law Operations

In some rural areas of England, during the late eighteenth century, changes occurred in the administration of the Poor Law which had significant repercussions.[17] Essentially, these changes increased the structure's reliance on formal enforcement procedures to control donors. The payments to poor persons made by local parishes had always been determined by two administrative forces: the judgments of local Justices of the Peace as to which persons were "poor" and what was "necessary" support, and the day-to-day decisions made by parish overseers of the poor. It was sometimes charged that the Justices of the Peace applied unrealistic standards, that they were too sympathetic to the pressures and pleas of the poor, while the elected overseers were liable to yield to their parishes' "soft-hearted" majority groups who, in reality, paid only a small fraction of the taxes levied.

In the late 1700's, an agricultural depression began to affect British rural society, and, in 1795, the Justices of the Peace in some counties adopted the principle that a poor person's welfare allotment should be based on the size of the applicant's family, and should be related to the price of bread. In effect, they created an inflation-adjusted guaranteed minimum income related to family size. This principle, called the Spleedham Rule (after the parish where it originated) was applied in many parts of England for about thirty years. Operationally, the rule meant that it might be rewarding for some heads of large rural families to become dependent paupers rather than support their own families through paid employment. In addition, paupers were assigned by parishes to work for regular employers who were then forgiven an equivalent amount of their taxes. This policy encouraged many employers to "employ" large numbers of paupers (who might work very inefficiently) as compared to using fewer competent paid workers to accomplish the same amount of work. There was also evidence that many local overseers of the poor were excessively liberal in permitting persons to qualify as paupers. Finally, the original Poor Law had envisioned that most paupers would be assigned to work under public supervision in a workhouse and live in a parish poorhouse. In practice, most paupers remained in their own homes and, where they were able to work, were assigned to regular employers who received tax rebates.

These policies were obviously preferred by the paupers and by many employers. And, in fact, they did sometimes lower the costs of Poor Law operation. But the policies also removed many of the deterrents that originally surrounded one's decision to beome an applicant for support by others. Modern scholars have estimated that, during the early nineteenth century, about ten percent of the population of Great Britain were receiving help through the Poor Law.[18] As can be imagined, this medley of developments was the subject of widespread controversy. Still, the core problems underlying the controversies were not simple. How much support should a "pauper" receive? Who should decide? What should be done if his family is so large that he "cannot" support such a family on a regular wage? What deterrents should confront an adult community member who asks to be regarded essentially as a donee? And what are the effects of pervasive "easy" welfare policies in shaping the socialization of young persons?

These issues had obvious implications for the genral operation of intercohort reciprocity systems. There are actually several themes running throughout these controversies. These themes were exemplified in the works and writings of Thomas Chalmers, first an economist and later a minister of the Presbyterian Church of Scotland.[19] At this point an extended discussion of Chalmers' activities and their implication can provide a useful basis for our later analyses.

Chalmers: Reviving Informal Systems

In the early nineteenth century, Chalmers was a minister in a rural Scottish parish near the Scotch/English border. The Poor Law did not operate in Scotland at that time. Chalmers observed a dramatic difference between the social and economic life of his Scottish parish and the neighboring English parishes. The Scots maintained a higher quality of community and family life, and children and adults evinced better personal character. He suspected that the operation of the Poor Law was a major cause of these differences. Chalmers concluded that the remote, formally enforced modes of reciprocity promoted by the Poor Law diminished proximate interdependence between social classes, and among community members, and undermined individual trust, initiative, and self respect.

He also realized that there was a significant difference between receiving donations from an immediate, local, informal institution (i.e., the local Scotch Presbyterian Church) composed of solicitous neighbors, and receiving donations ultimately raised by a process of formal taxation. Essentially, the dependent donee who benefitted through informally enforced donations from immediate neighbors can recognize the limited nature of the resources available, and be appropriately inhibited and grateful as a result of such knowledge. Conversely, when the donations come through a formally mediated enforcement process, donees tend to feel that the amount of taxable resources is almost infinite, and that symptoms of discontent and suffering are required in order to wring more money out of this remote and impersonal resource. Chalmers contended that the satisfaction provided to dependent donees by assistance is largely determined by the process of collection and donation, and not so much by the amount donated; when the government becomes the mediator, the aspirations of many donees are uncontrollably inflated.

Because of his concern with the psychology of donation, Chalmers also analyzed other aspects of the emotional exchanges that occur between donors and donees, especially in informally enforced exchanges in immediate reciprocity systems. He perceived that such exchanges, as compared to formally enforced ones, inevitably had far more emotional richness. Donors and donees in informal exchanges were both obviously engaged in affecting one another's attitudes and they both received quick feedback. However, in formally enforced exchanges, the independent donor's emotional responses are shaped by some abstract body of attitudes about social obligations, or by hostile opinions about tax collectors, or by the rapacity of certain indeterminate poor persons; the dependent donee may be principally stimulated to provoke guilt (and thus generosity) in the remote and invisible body politic. Chalmers observed that pleas from donees, in situations involving potential informal donations, might provoke a variety of responses from independent donors: appeals to the donees' pride; words of encouragment or advice; acts of sympathy and faith; the delivery of donations; or even caustic or scornful remarks. Ultimately, the emotional context of such immediate exchanges probably becomes more important than their obviously material elements. But this panoply of transactional machinery is abandoned when the donees' request is directed to a remote, formally enforced reciprocity network. Obviously, the remarks made in an earlier chapter about multiple-purpose transactions are pertinent here.

Chalmers determined to attempt an experiment to test his theories. In 1819, he became minister of the parish of St. John's, the largest and poorest parish in the industrial city of Glasgow, Scotland, with 10,000 parishioners. By this time, the Poor Law was in operation in that city. Under its provisions, funds raised via taxes levied in the entire city were pooled among the parishes for relief. Chalmers, after much controversy, got his parish exempted from the distribution of those funds. He proposed that the needy members of the parish be supported exclusively from funds raised by informally enforced (i.e., "voluntary") contributions by their co-parishioners. Twenty-five uncompensated deacons were appointed for the parish, one for each potentially dependent fifty families. The first responsibility of each deacon was to become acquainted with his charges, and make known his interest in their welfare. If parish members had difficulties, deacons used every means to provide counsel and encouragement, and to stimulate relatives and neighbors to take equivalent steps. An offer of material aid from the parish, collected from the poor to help the poor, was made only as a last measure. Every possible step was taken to encourage the potential dependent donee to perceive of himself as an active member of a network of reciprocity, not as someone receiving a donation because of a theoretic entitlement. Chalmers reported that the system was so successful that it prompted poor persons from elsewhere in the city to move to his parish (even though its total level of relief distribution was lower than other parishes in the city) because they preferred its humane and personal approach. In a typical report, one of his deacons described his mode of operation. He observed that

> each deacon may invite the sympathy of neighbors
> towards persons in distress, and thereby provide
> for the sufferers in a far more ample manner than
> by a parish contribution. A case in my district

of a poor woman, long under a lingering illness,
and which terminated in her death, might be ad-
duced to show how much even of comfort sometimes atises out of private charity. This person was
unable, for a considerable time, to maintain her-
self by her own earnings, and yet no desire was
manifested for parish aid; the neighbors, and those
that had heard of her situation, came forward on
her behalf, so she appeared to stand in need of
nothing that was necessary.[20]

Despite its conspicuous success, the system gradually declined in
vitality because of two administrative barriers that Chalmers had never
been able to remove. The parish, though it receive no income from
the city-wide Poor Law funds, was still taxed to contribute to that
pool. Thus it really was "taxed" twice. Furthermore, the parish could
not establish its own law of settlement and restrict the right of
other persons to move into its jurisdiction. As a result, the more
successfully the system operated, the greater the drain on its resources.
Eventually, these barriers led the parishioners to abandon the experiment.

It is evident that Chalmers tried to recreate in his urban neighborhood many of the informal, immediate, continuous elements that
sustained effective rural reciprocity systems. His (qualified) success,
and his many writings, served as a stimulant to later nineteenth
century leaders concerned with designing and sustaining systems of
informally enforced donations.[21] But, as we will see, perhaps because
some of these leaders were more secular in their perspective, and
operated in multi-religious environments, they were reluctant to propose the recreation of bounded communities, such as a church
parish, which had been central to Chalmers' system.

The Psychology of Giving and Receiving

Chalmers' observations on the styles of some of the local opponents of his experiment were not only colorful and perceptive, but
they also characterized two important intellectual themes underlying
attitudes toward donations to the poor and helpless. As we will see,

these themes are still highly relevant in our post-industrial society. Let us read his words, and then consider their fuller implications. First, he described the businesslike, rational view of the problem. "The community of Glasgow was vigorous, active, and in many ways intellectual; but above all it was a mercantile community. Any scheme in which figures were duly set down and balanced against results to be attained, they could understand and appreciate.... But they were singularly blind to the merits of a process founded in the study of human nature, and to the far more solid results attainable by indirect methods. Hence their preference for a cut and dried system — so many paupers, so many thousand pounds a year; hence their choice for State relief, rather than moral force...."[22] Then, he described the proponents of active, vigorous charity: "An equally determined opposition was encountered from another party of an opposite temperament, namely, the short-sighted advocates of humanity, pure and simple. They were personified by Dr. Shorter...a mere lump of benevolence...he was unable to see anything beyond the immediate symptoms of want and suffering.... Above all he could not bear to wait for any gradual improvement...."[23]

The rational, businesslike opponents of Chalmers' approach exemplified philosophic themes that were identified and discussed by Henry Maine in the mid-nineteenth century. Maine observed that societies had been steadily tending to move from relationships determined by status to relationships determined by legal contracts.[23] This tendency could also be characterized as a shift from informal enforcement of continuous transactions to formal enforcement of discrete transactions. Maine was largely concerned with the commercial and economic implications of this shift. However, the shift also had significance for the structuring of the systems for donations. There was general agreement in England that, despite the decline in status-based relations, a society could not leave its "dependents" to starve, or to grow up uneducated. A tendency grew to apply the commercial model described by Maine to the donation process: that is, to tax independent donors and thus use formal enforcement; to distribute funds to technically eligible donees in discrete transactions that did not involve serious emotional interchange (as in a commercial sale); and finally to conclude that nothing was due back from the donee, even as some ordinary commercial transaction might not be profitable.

Presumably, it was this model that shaped the responses of some of the business leaders described by Chalmers.

The complexities engendered by the "benevolent" approach to donations were somewhat more elaborate than those generated by a businesslike approach. Some of these were touched on earlier in the discussion on altruism and volition; however, the perspectives developed by Chalmers add to the previous analysis.

Chalmers' focus was on the *psychology* of reciprocity in general, and charity in particular: exactly what happens when particular human beings are routinely placed in the category of donors or donees? However, there is also the matter of the *philosophy* of reciprocity and charity: how *should* people feel in such situations? Really, Chalmers' psychology was not too different from the ideas discussed by Aristotle or Seneca. Of course, to Aristotle and Seneca, psychology and philosophy were inextricably mingled. But, gradually, over many centuries a *philosophy* of charity began to evolve. This philosophy eventually influenced the operation of certain reciprocity systems.

The developing philosophy of charity gave increasing weight to the motives and obligations of independent donors. Thus, in the first century, Paul the Apostle, in his letter to the Corinthians, counseled his converts that "If I bestow all my goods to feed the poor, and then I give my body to be burned, and have not charity, it profiteth me nothing." The rationale of Paul's statement, and of his continuing eloquent praise of charity, is quite pertinent. Paul was called the Apostle of the Gentiles and was identified as the carrier of the message of Christ — who was formally a Jew — to persons who were not Jews. In effect, Paul was striving to broaden a network of reciprocity. Perhaps these aims stimulated him to focus increasingly on the motives of donors rather than on the interrelationships between independent donors and dependent donees. After all, a focus on such motives might stimulate donors to be active within increasingly extended reciprocity networks, (such as might be operative in an international church) where their contacts with the donees might be limited or even unrewarding. But such extended networks might still be viable if donors constantly focused on their own personal motives and attitudes. We must also recognize that Paul's pleas to the congregation in Corinth was directed to a body of perhaps a few hundred persons. He was largely concerned with stimulating charity among the members of this small group, and possibly between these members and occasionally visiting Christians. In other words, while Paul's language was general, its context implies the scope of his aims was quite narrow.

Of course, the Bible presents a variety of perspectives on the immensely complex issue of reciprocity; thus, as the quote in Chapter 2 suggests, the theme of heavenly reward for donors has been important, while some religious commentators have discussed the responsibility of donors to distribute their gifts so as to produce the maximum benefits to others.[25] Still, the Pauline themes combined both a poetic and practical appeal. What persons might not occasionally like to be surrounded by a pool of persons who donated without making reciprocal demands? Further, an institution that evolved into a *catholic* church could have far-reaching operations facilitated by a membership that contributed without excessive reciprocal demands. Over the centuries, the appeal of Paul's approach attracted increasing number of supporters. Eventually, the eighteenth century philosopher Immanuel Kant epitomized many of these trends in his articulation of the concept of the categorical imperative. That concept proposed that individuals should assess their own conduct solely in terms of its relationships to general principles, rather than in terms of the responses it provokes from others. As a result of these growing influences, the concept of *charity* — of giving without recompense in any form — gradually assumed prominence over the concept of reciprocity.

This shift in perspective can be demonstrated by changes in literary fashions. Thus Seneca, a "pagan" philosopher, discussed reciprocity as evidence of the noble and humane virtue of fellowship. In contrast, consider the approach of the Duke de la Rochefoucauld, a seventeenth century French nobleman, who wrote a book of social maxims.[26] The book included many references to the obligation of reciprocity. But Rochefoucauld's maxims, despite their psychological acuity, discussed reciprocity in almost pornographic overtones; it seemed as if it were improper to recognize publicly that donations create obligations, that donors do and should consider the likelihood that they will be compensated, and that failure to reciprocate can have serious consequences for the donees. In effect, the *philosophy* of reciprocity, symbolized by a banner emblazoned with the word "Charity" was beginning to drive its *psychology* underground. Undoubtedly, it was the vigorous — if sometimes unstructured — enthusiasms that charity mobilized which provoked Chalmers' remark about a "lump of benevolence."

The persistent "modern" focus on benevolence — on the attitudes of donors in charitable situations — justifies, at this point, an explicit analysis of the "forgotten" element of such acts — the attitudes of dependent donees. This analysis must be based on psychological principles. Essentially, a donee who receives something he values from a donor is presented with a significant challenge. The act of benevolence automatically creates a form of implicit dependency for the donee.[27] The gift, by definition, is desirable or valuable. As a result the donee is inevitably prone to speculate how he can win further equivalent donations — if there has been one valuable donation, there is naturally the possiblity of more. Such speculation is a form of dependency, which may range in intensity from vague aspirations to desperate reliance.[28] Eventually, the dependent donee realizes that the best way to obtain further donations is to engage in some form of conduct — a counterdonation — that will provoke more gifts. The counterdonation may be simple economic repayment, or acts of gratitude, or self-abnegation. But the donee may find the appropriate reciprocal acts either impossible or distasteful: then, he must either abandon his expectations (i.e., his dependency), or devise substitutions for the traditional reciprocal responses. Abandoning expectations is always painful, which explains why many gifts — where there cannot be effective counterdonations — create more anxiety and resentment than joy. Thus, much of the donee's psychic energy is often directed toward the devising of substitute (i.e., less painful) reciprocal acts, to continue the flow of donations. One such substitute is for the donee to stimulate guilt or fear in the independent donor, and lead him to believe that such discomfort can be dissipated by further donations. In effect, the dissipation of the donor's guilt becomes the donee's counterdonation to the donor. Once again, reciprocity has been established, and the painful dependency of the donee has been corrected.

Now, many donors realize that it is not in anyone's interest to "teach" dependent donees to try to stimulate guilt or fear. But in some situations donees are inevitably in persisting dependency (e.g., children, the aged). The dependent donees will naturally seek to moderate their dependency by creating exchanges. Seneca, Rochefoucauld, and Chalmers were especially concerned with analyzing the problems of these donees. Essentially, they felt that where donees could not provide donors with material reciprocity, the donees could still engage in *symbolic* reciprocity; that, under appropriate circumstances, the donee's words and acts of deference and gratitude could constitute "repayment," and increase the donee's potency. Undoubtedly, these acts of deference and gratitude were what Chalmers had in mind when he discussed the "moral" problems of poor relief. Where he remarked about preserving the "dignity" of donees, our contemporary vocabulary would talk about devising structures and expectations that encouraged donees to symbolically "earn" their assistance, and thus still escape debilitating dependency. Of course, Chalmers' words — "morality" and "dignity" — present the issue with greater force than does the abstract terminology of transactional analysis.

It is true that donors may devise other means — beyond the stimulation of deference or gratitude — of dealing with the burdens of dependency that benevolence creates for the resourceless donee. Donors can clearly define and articulate the limits of their donations at early stages in the donation process. The definition may be an irrevocable commitment to donate a specific amount and no more, or it may be an offer to donate a specific amount if certain conditions are met (i.e., if reciprocity is practiced), but that no more than the predetermined amount will be donated under any conditions. Such a definition — if it is clear and immutable — can inform donees that their dependency must be limited, and that no conduct by them can alter that situation. This message, if it is believed by donees, can free them from excessive dependency — whether the dependency is demonstrated by gratitude, deference, or even grossly destructive conduct. Unfortunately, it is not always easy for independent donors to make such precise, permanent, and speedy decisions about the parameters of a situation inviting donations: after all, one can not automatically predict when the actual causes of a donee's incapacity will expire.

Another technique sometimes applied by donors — to free donees of dependency — is the posture of infinite benevolence (i.e., the posture implied in Chalmers' reference to a "mere lump of benevolence"). In other words, donors can contend that their beneficence in infinite, and that donees should never fear their potential dependency will be unsatisfied. If donees truly believe this, they may accept extraordinary dependency with equanimity. But the proposition that there are infinite resources is preposterous, as donees eventually realize. And even donors who utter such words will eventually take them back. Furthermore, if available resources are large, donees will be tempted to expand their demands, both to test reality, and because the potential for human demands is — as we know — quite expansive. In any case, for better or worse, and for a variety of reasons (some of which we will discuss later), the benevolence approach, with its implicit disregard for the psychic needs of the donee, steadily gathered popular support throughout the industrial era. Now, after this digression to develop some essential themes, let us return to our chronology.

Old Age in the Early Industrial Revolution

Throughout the nineteenth century, the Industrial Revolution developed apace in both England and America. The Revolution did not automatically extinguish previous patterns of intercohort reciprocity. In some early English textile mills, for example, employers deliberately hired whole families to work machines, treating the parents as supervisors of their children — just as those parents might have earlier worked under their own parents' supervision on a farm.[29] Naturally, such a structure provided strong support for patterns of intrafamily cohort exchanges. Other employers, for benevolent and material reasons (and I do not believe it is wise to deny that persons classed as employers are any more incapable of benevolence than ministers, politicians or teachers), maintained "paternalistic systems," which provided the employees with much more than contract-defined material benefits, and for which the employers hoped, among other things, to be repaid with reciprocal loyalty.

Still, as Maine had noted, the Revolution did gradually increase the proportion of person-to-person, contract-based relationships. One effect of such change was to place growing numbers of urban industrial workers — who were cut off from the support of proximate villagers — in fear of isolation and pauperism (an especially distressing form of dependency) in their old age. Furthermore, the workers might even lack the personal resources to assure they received a decent burial. As a response to such threats, a new mediating system, the so-called "friendly societies," began to appear in urban England in the late eighteenth century.[30] The societies were actually insurance clubs, whose members paid (donated) periodic dues, and who were promised support (counterdonations) from the club in case of predefined emergencies, sickness, or death. However, there were significant contrasts between such groups and modern insurance companies. The societies, perhaps harkening back to the rural traditions and the need for symbolic ties, gave a great deal of weight to *social* — as well as *economic* — reciprocity among their members. There were annual membership banquets, monthly meethings, bands, parades, and other symbols of affiliation. One motive for such activities was to recruit additional members, so as to increase the stability of the societies' capital, but the simple pleasure of fellowship was obviously equally important. In other words, the societies were multi-purpose entities. However, the fellowship motivation, although it assisted recruiting, did create significant tensions in some societies. Inevitably, issues arose about what proportion of the funds of such societies should be dedicated to "fellowship" purposes and what should be saved and distributed as economic benefits.

Another problem facing the societies was the primitive level of actuarial knowledge existing at that time. The quality of this knowledge was so low that the societies could not accurately compute the level of payments necessary to provide predetermined death benefits for a club with a specified age composition. Reliable actuarial tables needed to make such computations just did not exist. Gradually some of the societies did grow in administrative sophistication (as actuarial knowledge increased) while others expired. But such growth usually meant the concomitant decline in their "friendly" purposes, as more resources were preserved to pay benefits, and technical staff set policies that constrained the pro-fraternal perspectives of local chapters (e.g., eligibility for admission was determined by actuarial criteria rather than social amicability). Ultimately, the insurance purposes initially served by friendly societies — both in England and America — were gradually taken over by the modern life and health insurance industry. This activity was a new form of single-purpose institution brought about by the Industrial Revolution, and which used the technology underlying that Revolution. It has been suggested that some of the entertainment purposes of the friendly societies have been supplemented by specialized, commercial entertainment presented via the mass media. Obviously, both these systems — insurance companies and commercial entertainment — may develop "products" of higher quality than the activities of friendly societies. Unfortunately, the new systems also transform active members into passive observers, and place these observers either in the middle of crowds of strangers, or alone in their homes. Perhaps we have replaced fellowship with entertainment.

Controversies About Helping Dependents

In Great Britain, during the early 1830's, a Royal Commission was established to investigate the general operation of the Poor Law and, particularly, the effect of the Spleedham Rule. The Commission's Report exhaustively criticized the current system for providing benefits and determining eligibility.[31] The *Report* recommended that parishes establish family benefit rates which (regardless of the size of the donees' family) were lower than those paid to individual wage laborers, and that paupers be required to live in a poorhouse and work in a workhouse maintained by the parish. These proposals aimed to keep pauperism so unattractive as to stimulate poor persons to seek employment and to manage their lives so as to avoid becoming paupers.

A modern economist, Mark Balug, in a careful analysis of the tabulations underlying the *Report*, concluded that (a) the scope of the undesirable practices, by the time the Commission went into operation, was much exaggerated, and (b) the effects supposedly attributed to the practices were due to a multiplicity of causes, many unrelated to the Poor Law.[32] Despite the apparent merit of Balug's analysis, the *Report* was highly influential. Many of its sympathetic readers feared the intensification of the tendencies the *Report* seemed to identify (i.e., the decline of vital reciprocal relationships), and were disposed to treat the *Report* as a caution, if not a revelation. Incidentally, Balug's analysis did not "disprove" the psychology of the assumptions about reciprocity underlying the *Report*; he simply showed that the data collected in the early 1830's did not sustain the charge that the policy of reciprocity was threatened at that particular time. The policy may have been threatened earlier, but that threat was moderated by administrative tightening-up (during the 1820's) in many parishes, and the policy might have been threatened later, but the possiblity of such a threat was eliminated by the impact of the *Report.*

Interestingly enough, a number of later commentators on poverty policy, perhaps more sympathetic to the aspirations of the poor than the Commissioners, conceded that there were numerous short-comings in the operation of the Law during the early 19th century.[33] However, these commentators attributed the deficiencies to primitive techniques of administration — which were allegedly endemic to the times — rather than to basic philosophical flaws in the operation of the Law, e.g., the Spleedham Rule. Implicitly, the answer to the shortcomings of "weak administration" was better-trained and more professional administration. Of course, the commentators were essentially trainers of social workers — the modern administrators of such statutes. In any event, the *Report* did not disavow society's "obligation" to help the poor. The issue was: what means would best attain this end? Throughout the nineteenth century, there was continuous controversy in both England and America about how to render this help.

The Persistence of Informal Enforcement

Private charity, collected through informal enforcement procedures, remained an important resource in both countries. Throughout the entire nineteenth century such donations were probably the principal means of providing assistance to all categories of dependent adults and youths. For example, in England, until 1870, most elementary schools for students from poorer families were supported by payments from parents, contributions from church members, and the services of adult volunteers.[34] Even in America, with its pattern of tax-supported schools, during the nineteenth century wealthy persons often made contributions to cover textbook purchases or to provide prizes in public elementary and high schools.[35] Cynical commentators have sometimes characterized these donations as inspired by guilt. But such attributions were often inaccurate. For instance,

John D. Rockefeller's personal account book, which he maintained throughout his life, revealed that, in 1855, at the age of 16 — when he first went to work — he began making frequent donations to charity. During much of his youth, these contributions equalled ten percent or more of his income.[36] And, throughout Rockefeller's whole life, he regularly taught Sunday School. Probably the "guilt" that provoke Rockefeller's benevolence had more to do with certain strains of Protestantism than with his business practices in adult life. Again, when Andrew Carnegie was a young immigrant boy, a wealthy citizen of Pittsburgh made his personal library available to youths in the community. Carnegie made extensive use of those books — and he had a bookish bent: he wrote four serious books in his adult life. Thus, it was obviously not only guilt that caused him to dedicate much of his fortune to founding free public libraries.[37] Finally, during the American Civil War, all the costs of maintaining and managing the medical, health, and sanitary services of the Union Army were provided not by taxes, but by the voluntary contributions of citizens.[38] It was assumed that the citizens of the North should make their own "voluntary" donations in exchange for the sacrifices of their fighting men.

Nineteenth century philanthropy gave greater stress to economic aid than was the case in earlier historic periods. However, the concept of personal engagement of the donor with the dependent donees was still vital — and was reinforced by the comparatively small size of the institutions involved. This reinforcement undoubtedly provided donors with powerful gratifications. For example, William Pryor Letchworth, a later nineteenth century businessman/philanthropist, included the following anecdote in a report he prepared on his efforts (in New York State) to have abandoned children removed from poorhouses, where they received inadequate care:

> At my request Dr. H. P. Wilber, the humane and intelligent Superintendent of the Asylum for Feebleminded Children, at Syracuse, came to Buffalo twice to examine children with reference to receiving some of them there [from the poorhouse]. Among those he took was a crippled boy, so deformed that he could not walk. His legs were

curled under his body, and he was obliged to sit
through the day on the floor. His only mode of
locomotion was by placing his hands on the floor
at right angles with his wrists and arms and lifting
himself along. He was not a bright boy, but fairly
intelligent. His case was a sad one, as his future
seemed pointed to a life in the poorhouse. Some
two years later, when I was visiting the institution
at Syracuse, as I stood in one of the classrooms, a
lad about twelve years old, with a bright, smiling
face, came to me from across the room, saying,
"How do you do, Mr. Letchworth," and advanced
to shake hands with me. Dr. Wilber said: "You do
not remember this boy. This is ———, the crippled
lad from the Erie County Poorhouse, who used to
walk with his hands." I learned that the efforts of
Dr. Wilber, assisted by physicians in Syracuse, had
enabled the boy to walk erect. In exercises at the
blackboard which I saw him take part in he did not
differ materially in appearance from the boys
around him. As I looked on his bright, happy face
and watched his natural movements I could not
but breathe a silent blessing on good Dr. Wilber.[39]

Of course, these many "voluntary" systems of reciprocity were
not without their informal means of enforcement. In England, the subscription list was a prominent device.[40] This list was a published
statement of the names and the status (e.g., titles) of persons prominently associated with particular donation campaigns. Each person listed
acquired a certain degree of recognition (a precious good) by reason
of such publication, and that recognition could be heightened by the
prominence of some of the persons listed as sponsors, and by statements as to the amount donated. Similarly, not to be listed on
particular subscription lists might threaten certain potential donors
with implicit acts of social retaliation. Another device sometimes used
in England was granting donors the authority to designate certain
dependent persons as beneficiaries of charitable institutions that they,
the donors, helped to endow.[41] For instance, in the case of a home

for elderly persons, since there might well be more applicants than slots available, sponsorship by one or more donors helped applicants attain priority. Of course, this process of "bidding," involving donors, applicants and institutions, might be deemed offensive. But, if donors were allegedly choosing where to place their money — which they had earned — what is so wrong with giving them some say in how it is to be spent? In any event, the spirit of the times assumed a vital interaction between donors and their donees.

Donations to Help the Young

Throughout the whole nineteenth century the number and proportion of young persons attending school steadily increased. Their time of school attendence simultaneously lengthened. In England, as noted, many of these schools were supported by informally enforced contributions. In America, tax funds (formally enforced contributions) were much more common. Still, it would be inaccurate to treat such tax-based funds as purely involuntary payments. The taxes were levied and collected because high proportions of American voters — from upper classes as well as poor groups — concluded that such schools were generally good for the society, and they supported candidates who proposed to levy taxes to support schools. Of course, different voters supported such legislation for different purposes — just as different persons "give" to charity for different reasons. But regardless of such diverse motives, the general principle was that voters supported such taxes because they believed that they, as individuals, would receive some reciprocal benefits in return. The future benefits could range from "repayment" in their afterlife to being able to hire more competent, better educated employees; but all such benefits constitute counterdonations. Interestingly enough, even in America, with its emphasis on tax support for its schools, public contributions (in the nineteenth century) were also common. Thus, many rural schools were managed by school boards that took an active part in school operations: interviewing teachers, visiting the school, or helping with repairs. Such unpaid involvement was a form of donation.

The donations of adults in shaping nineteenth century youth policy — as well as their day-to-day donations in carrying out these policies — also warrant consideration. In all societies, significant proportions of the time of some able adults must be spent in planning the design and maintenance (as well as operation) of youth environments that will produce socialization to reciprocity. In other words, the innumerable micro-decisions about how to raise children made by parents and persons in immediate contact with the young must — especially during periods of general change — be supplemented by longer-range, "policy" oriented decisions made by adults with larger responsibilities and authority. The nineteenth century was surely a time of such general change. And, during the era, many competent adults — both in England and America — dedicated large proportions of their time to affecting youth policy. Their activities touched on policies relating to child labor, the public schools, the planning of settlement houses, the role of philanthropy, and the prevention of juvenile delinquincy. Many of these adults were uncompensated volunteers (often members of the upper-middle class). In effect, their donation of time was an instance of informally enforced reciprocity. Presumably, in exchange for these donations, they hoped to see a better society, or to preserve what they currently saw as valuable.[42] Possibly, they saw themselves participating in the Great Exchange.[43] Of course, this reliance on informally enforced donations provoked certain frustrations for planning efforts: volunteers could not always be held to the same commitments nor expected to undertake the same arduous training as paid professionals. On the other hand, the economic security of the volunteer's family was not dependent on his retaining his "helping" job, nor on enlarging the budget of his institution. This is not to contend that volunteers never develop overidentification with their "causes." However, it is still likely that such overidentification is more likely when the donations of helpers are tangibly reciprocated with salaries, rather than intangible, observable, constructive changes in the conduct of the donees.

During the nineteenth century, formal education brought about through the donations of adults still absorbed only a small proportion of the time of dependent young persons. Youths who went to school still spent most of their time in contact with non-school adults — often outside their immediate family — who assisted in their socialization process. These adults were employers, shopkeepers, neighbors,

Sunday school teachers, and more remote relatives. (Recall the story about Carnegie and his friends being lent books.) All of them were, in effect, contributing their time and energy (their most precious resources) to assist the next cohorts to grow up in a healthy fashion. Sometimes the adults — e.g., employers of the young — were economically aided for their efforts, and sometimes their efforts were explicit donations. Still, even the employers often had independent relations with the parents of their young employees and undertook their hiring and socialization partly as a consideration to the parents.[44] Or, again, these employers often managed very small businesses, where the relationship of adult and youth might involve many elements of intimacy. Thus, employers were often motivated by considerations beyond direct profit: sometimes, unquestionably, these supplementary motives must have extended into the realm of intercohort donations, motivated by the natural desire to help shape a youth into a future effective adult, who might someday come back and say "Thank you." Then too, some of these employers also must have hoped that their donations might stimulate other persons in the community to give reciprocal considerations to their own children. Inevitably, as the time spent in school increased, the scope of these informally enforced adult donations diminished, and the scope of their formally enforced donations (via school taxes) enlarged.

Amateurs and Professionals: Generalists vs. Specialists

The general concern with interactions between independent donors and dependent donees culminated in the organization, in the late nineteenth century, of many "Charity Organization" societies in both England and America.[45] These societies represented a movement to maintain a central role for non-professional workers and informally enforced donations in the field of helping activities. One important motive for their thrust was the theme articulated by Chalmers — that personal engagement between the donors and donees was necessary to prevent the giving process from being corroded with destructive forces. Another major force was the ideology of Pauline charity, which essentially perceived charity as a personal, loving, and voluntary (i.e., informally enforced) act: obviously, charitable donations lose some of these personal elements when they are transmitted through bureaucratic, governmental mediating agencies. Finally, these societies were influenced by the concepts of Social Darwinism, which attained great influence during the last half of the nineteenth century.[46]

Social Darwinism held that traits learned by members of one generation might be biologically transferred to their descendants. The prestige of Social Darwinism was greatly enhanced by the growing acceptance of Darwin's genetic doctrines: indeed, Darwin, himself, accepted the essence of Social Darwinism, though it was admittedly not central to his basic doctrine. Social Darwinsim implied that "bad traits" — crime, alcoholism — learned by one generation could be quickly and inevitably genetically transmitted to succeeding generations. And poor persons, who frequently displayed such traits, tended to have larger families than more "responsible" persons. As a result, the fear arose that society might speedily find itself overwhelmed by generations with the "bad" bred into them. The anxieties created by Social Darwinism provoked large proportions of upper-middle class persons — partly as an act of self-protection — to engage themselves in the management of help to the poor. These independent donors favored helping systems that encouraged serious engagement between donors and donees, since their motives were not only to sustain poor people, but to change the way they lived (or raised their children). These diverse motives were articulated through the Charity Organization societies — which, at first, aimed not so much to distribute charity, but to place potential donors and donees in touch with one another.

The Advance of the Professionals

As the urban, industrial society enlarged, the demands on Charity Organization societies increased. The comparative anonymity of large cities encouraged some needy applicants to apply to several potential donors, and often to conceal from each agency or private donor the help he was receiving from others. Thus, the societies evolved into clearinghouses for agencies and donors. Then, as economic depressions occasionally occurred — with increasing intensity as the size of the urban industrial work force enlarged — donors periodically found themselves faced with the unique phenomenon of large numbers of relatively competent, healthy adults who could not support themselves because of the lack of paid work. (In contrast, in an agricultural environment, such persons could "tighten their belts" and still, perhaps, raise enough food to feed their families.) The challenge of industrial unemployment increased the demands placed on charity. And of course, such unemployment — and the other social tensions associated with industrial work — increased the level of worker unionization. In the longer run, unions fostered greater reliance on formal systems of governmentally enforced donations (though, at first, union support of government action was far greater in England that America — evidently American unions were still affected by the American tradition of independence).[47]

Another novel challenge facing the Charity Organization societies was the Demographic Revolution. The tremendous increases in affluence, medical knowledge, and health producing systems (i.e., modern sanitation) brought about by the Industrial Revolution dramatically lowered the human death rate over about 150 years, starting about 1800.[48] By the early nineteenth century, the average life span was between 30 to 40 years in Europe and America. But, by 1850, when the male life span in Massachusetts averaged 38 years, a male at the age of 20 had a life expectation of 40 more years. By 1976, the American life expectation for males was 69 years, and a male at the age of 20 had a life expectation of 51.6 years. One effect of these changes was to dramatically increase the number of persons surviving into old age. Thus, in 1880, 3.4% of Americans were age 65 or older; by 1940, the figure had doubled to 6.8%. The impact of such survival was further intensified by the increasing proportion of persons engaged in industrial work.

In a farm environment, as a worker's effectiveness declined with aging, it was possible to restructure his work so as to enable him to slow down yet remain productively engaged. In industrial work, such partial retirement was more difficult to organize. As a result, the proportion of industrial workers who continued working in their old age tended to be much lower than the proportion of rural workers. Thus, in 1900, when many American workers were still employed on farms, 63% of the males over 65 were members of the labor force (and almost all of them self-employed); in 1960, only 32% of the males over 65 were in the labor force — although the absolute number of males over 65, and their proportion in comparison to other age groups, have both increased.[49] As a result of the Demographic and Industrial Revolutions, new systems for the care of the aged had to be developed — especially since this increasing population tended to live in urban environments, where family support networks were less viable than in many rural areas.

Support for the Charity Organization — or volunteer — approach was further eroded by scientific research finds that rejected the premises of Social Darwinism. Putting it baldly, the research demonstrated that if one trained a generation of rats to run mazes — or to be addicted to drugs — and did not similarly train a control group, the next generation of rats born to both the experimental and control groups — if removed from their mothers at birth — would display equal dispositions to run mazes or be addicted to drugs. In other words, acquired traits were not inheritable. Biologically, each generation starts from the same place as its parents. The process of evolution, this research found, depends not on the genetic inheritance of knowledge or skills, but on the tendency of the process to "natural selection." By this process, genetically ill-adapted persons, over many generations, tend to live shorter lives, and thus their descendants are slowly outnumbered by the descendants of longer-lived persons with better adapted genetic characteristics. These genetic discoveries naturally corroded the appeal of Social Darwinism.

However, Social Darwinism was also implicitly based on a more general — and more commonsense — approach that actually antedated the work of Darwin. Social Darwinism said that, in general, parents with "bad" habits are more disposed to rear "bad" children than are parents with "good" habits. The correctness of this proposition has been demonstrated innumerable times by modern sociology. This is not to say that children of bad parents are always, or even often, bad; however, it does say that poor homes and environments do make the future of children more problematic than good homes and environments. This proposition is not the same as that presented by Social Darwinism; Social Darwinism said that a child removed from a poor environment immediately after birth would still inherit a tendency toward "depravity." In contrast, sociological research has concluded that it is not the developed genetic inheritance, but rather the continuous bad influence around the child as it matures, which teaches it to be bad. If the child were removed at the point of birth, he would have no more tendency toward depravity than is found in most persons. But, as a practical matter, we can remove only a few children from their parents at the instant of birth, so whether the tendency toward depravity is genetic or learned, we arrive at the same point: children born in bad environments are more prone to become bad than are children born elsewhere, and it behooves society to become closely engaged in their upbringing. This was the central operational tenet of the "defeated" doctrine of Social Darwinism.

A final element shaping, and perhaps ultimately corrupting, the operations of the Charity Organization societies was the increasing secularization and professionalization of the donation process. These trends developed because the growing need for charity enlarged the scope of their operations. Such need stimulated the development of larger and more governmentally-based institutions which often tended to model themselves after the successful private business agencies spreading throughout the society. Obviously, government agencies in pluralistic societies would tend toward secularization. Some leaders in charity organizations supported these trends toward "scientific," professionalized charity, while others criticized the erosion of the personal relationship between donor and donees.[50] The "New Professionals" did not deprecate the need for personal relations, but contended that contacts between academically trained professionals and donees were more productive than donor-to-donee contacts.

This conflict between the amateurs and professionals extended over perhaps forty years — from about 1880 to 1920. Of course, the terms "amateur" and "professional" would not have been quite appropriate during that period, since both the amateurs and professionals had largely received their training on-the-job, and some of the amateurs headed substantial administrative enterprises. Still, the amateurs, in much the same traditions as Chalmers, were concerned with: informal enforcement; volunteer, unpaid workers; and the maintenance of intense — often "morally founded" — relationships between donors and donees. The professionals envisaged reliance on: formal enforcement (tax collected funds); paid workers; and, of necessity, the image of the donations as a secular act. The professional desperately aspired to couple the donation with effective counseling for donees, but as we will see, complex social forces tended to frustrate that aspiration.

How Should Widows Be Helped?

The widow's pensions movement provides an excellent example of the course of these amateur/professional tensions. During the late nineteenth century in America, proposals were made to provide tax-supported pensions to needy widowed mothers. The payments would permit the mothers to maintain their children at home, so they would not be compelled to rely on the uncertain help of relatives, or to leave their homes and reside in the poorhouse, or to go out to work. One analogy given in support of the proposal was the elaborate existing network of aid offered to Civil War veterans and their families by the federal and state governments.

The "amateurs," the Charity Organization leaders, opposed the legislation. They contended that such mothers were already amply assisted by private charities whenever real need was demonstrated — and that personalized assistance was far more desirable than impersonal government aid. Furthermore, without personalized aid, there was a danger that such funds might be spent for "undeserving mothers." The "professionals," the proponents of the legislation, argued that private agencies had insufficient funds to meet their responsibilities, and that adequate safeguards could be established to insure that public funds were not spent to assist immoral persons, i.e., mothers of illegitimate children. The following quote represents a typical statement on behalf of voluntary charity, made in 1913 in objection to the movement:

> I cannot forbear to warn my friends who would lightly discard charity utterly from human society, that they are building upon the sand: that when they put their reliance entirely upon a self-contained, coercive system in which all the relief funds are raised by taxation and all are distributed arbitrarily or a per capita plan without reference to individual circumstances, without reference to

the thrift or efforts of the individual, without reference to the cooperation of relatives, of trade unions, of churches, or neighbors, without reference to any charitable agencies or social sources, they are making a violent break with the historical evolution of human society, they are following a will-of-the-wisp.

They are just now having a heyday of popularity. Many laws they have secured, and others are on the way.

As a student of social economy, I am much interested in these explanations. As a progressive and radical social reformer, I deeply regret the painful steps which we shall certainly have to retrace.[51]

On the other hand, at the same time proponents of the movement offered arguments of the following tenor:

The idea that...the relief given to widows is charity, is one of the worst handicaps...because the most self-respecting widows, the widows whom you want to help, will not accept it, because their children would become dependents on the rich.

Surely all of us, whatever may be our conception of "social justice," believe that the child must not be left to the care of the charitable, but has a right to be protected and cared for by the State. Every stage of progress in child-caring has met with this same objection from well-intentioned philanthropists. Public school, public libraries, public textbooks, public school lunches were all attained over this same sort of opposition. Strange as it seems, we are told that the "brotherhood of man" ceases at the very point when all men as brothers united democratically to help their children, and is only developed when the few help the many through "charity."

This conception is a relic of the days when to be charitable was a religious duty when it was sincerely believed that the poor were created that the fortunate might attain holiness by graciously granting relief to their humble brothers.

[Opponents of widow's pension legislation] would improve the situation by whipping up the businessman in his capacity as a philanthropist. But why not whip up the same man in his capacity as taxpayer? From his own standpoint, incidentally, and for the good of his own soul, since he has to pay the bill anyway, and ought to pay it, he should do it in the manner least calculated to tempt him toward thinking that he is performing an act of moral grandeur when he is really performing an act of elementary civic routine.[52]

Between 1910 and 1925, forty-four American states did pass legislation providing state and county funds for the at-home support of widowed mothers. The legislation in some of the states went further, (despite the arguments offered earlier by some of the professionals) and also provided support for the mothers of illegitimate children.[53] Up until the Great Depression in the early 1930's, the actual number of mothers assisted by such programs throughout America was comparatively small. Presumably, the size of the program was constrained by some of the inhibitions on aiding mothers of illegitimate children, the moral tone which still colored the administration of many governmental programs, the embarrasment felt by many eligible persons about admitting indigency (and becoming solely donees), and the localized roots of many administrators and their tax funds. The widowed mother statutes eventually became the framework of the Federal Aid to Families of Dependent Children program. By 1977, 11.8% of American children below 18 years of age (and their parent(s)) lived in families receiving assistance under this program. Seventy-nine percent of these children were eligible due to the absence of their father from the home (because of illegitimacy, divorce, or separation), and 31% of all eligible children lived in homes where the mother had never been married. Only 3.7% of the children were eligible due to their mother's widowhood. The annual costs of the program were over 10.1 billion dollars.[54]

In America, World War I was a major stimulus for shifting the nature of informal economic donations. The immense public support of the War brought about many fund raising drives to assist the welfare of men in the armed forces.[55] The provision of such assistance was complicated because many servicemen were overseas, outside the regular areas serviced by existing welfare organizations. Inevitably, pressures arose to coordinate and centralize the various fund drives, in order to lower costs and assist efficient planning. The consolidated drives that developed raised large amounts of money, which were allocated among participating agencies by predetermined formulas. These activities brought about the creation of an enlarged class of fund raising specialists, skilled in the elaborate planning underlying such drives. Eventually, the wartime drives encouraged the growth of other forms of consolidated fund raising in local communities. Such activities increased the segregation between donors, fund collectors, paid professional employees of charity agencies, and the ultimate recipients of assistance. As a result, even in many instances of informally enforced exchanges, contacts between donors and donees became increasingly remote.[56]

A Restatement

Our chronology is now approaching the era of the Great Depression. This is a good point for a brief summarization. Perhaps the most remarkable element of the previous chronology is that, while it covers about 250 years of dynamic social and economic development, most donations to help the young, old, or poor during the period were routinely transformed into immediate, continuous, informally enforced exchanges. (The one apparent exception to this proposition — the American public school — is specifically discussed below.) In other words, until the opening years of the Great Depression — as we will see — the majority of poor persons in America receiving public support were assisted by private donations rather than tax collected funds. Many intercohort donations — which were typically shaped into exchanges — occurred in the family, but others depended on more generalized philanthropic activities. Of course, there was, throughout the period, substantial reliance on the Great Exchange: many long-range donations of goods, self-gratification, and life were made by young persons, as well as others. However, this class of remote, indirect, informally enforced exchanges was part of a continuum of increasingly complex exchanges surrounding youths and adults. In effect, there was a series of successive, incremental transactional steps through which persons passed in becoming fully socialized to reciprocity. It is true that the later steps were rather abstract. But, through most of the period, large-scale, remote, formally enforced exchanges were but a small portion of social and economic exchanges.

The general pattern of informally enforced large-scale exchanges among independent donors and dependent donees was complimented by the persistence of patterns of informally enforced immediate exchanges among cohorts. Thus, in the case of the aged, as late as 1920, 48% of the American population lived in rural areas; families in such areas usually continued to treat older persons as active, contributing members; at the same time, the elderly were allowed to slow down their rate of contribution. In urban areas, the maintenance of such immediate exchanges with the aged was more complicated. Still, urban labor markets were more flexible (than now), and there was a lower proportion of aged persons. Thus, the number of aged persons not being given adequate assistance constituted a small fraction of society. As for the young, the comparatively high proportion of the population living in rural areas, the many household chores existing in both rural and urban environments, the large families typical of the period (generating child-caring-for-child chores), and the higher levels of youth employment all served to stimulate the young of most American families to be engaged actively in reciprocal exchanges within their families and neighborhoods.

We must recognize that there is one American institution that has practiced large-scale, remote, formally enforced intercohort reciprocity for a comparatively long period of time. This institution is the public school. Adult donors (i.e., taxpayers) to the schools have always hoped to receive reciprocal donations from the students, but (in industrial and post-industrial society) they expect those donations will occur during the adult life of the students. The remoteness of these counterdonations has been steadily attenuated by a number of circumstances. School and college have become increasingly prolonged, and so students stay in passive, non-contributing roles for longer periods of time. Educational institutions have become larger, more affluent and bureaucratic: as a result, it is harder for students to assist actively in the maintenance or operation of the buildings, or to contribute otherwise (i.e., counterdonate) to the school program. Furthermore, the increased rationalization and legalistic individualization of the school has made it more difficult for adults to socialize students to engage in acts of symbolic deference (to the adult-supported reciprocity systems that sustain the school), and thus to diminish their impotent dependence by presenting counterdonations. And, finally, the extra-student roles of young persons, where they might be expected to act as donors, as well as donees, have generally declined. In sum, the effect of the reciprocity systems surrounding contemporary public schools and colleges on the attitudes and values of our young is problematic. Some evidence about this effect will be presented later in the book. However, at this moment, we can merely note that the school reciprocity systems that existed around 1930 were not the same as those existing in 1977 — but they were more powerful, immediate, and informal. In fact, the school reciprocity systems that existed in, let us say, 1900, were even more powerful, immediate, and informal than those in 1930.

In considering the general effects of socialization to intercohort reciprocity, we must also recognize the imact of cultural lag. The most potent persons in any society — whether they are corporation presidents, politicians, professors, or newspaper editors — are typically between the ages of 45 to 65. These persons received their basic socialization to reciprocity twenty to forty years ago. Thus, at any point in time, the attitudes of this potent class toward reciprocity reflect the operation of the socialization system some years back. If the current socialization system is not effectively socializing the young toward reciprocity, the full effect of such negligence will not be felt until twenty to forty years hence, when those poorly socialized youths attain the peak of their generational power.

Despite the persistence of informally enforced reciprocity, it is also true that many modernizing (should one say "progressive"?) trends have subjected that system to continuous and growing pressures for change. The two disparate themes of (a) rational charity, and (b) benevolence, both identified by Chalmers in Glasgow in the early 1800's, have asserted their influence with growing frequency. Rational charity implicitly says, "You meet the legal definition of poor, so take this money, and go away and do not bother me." Benevolence says, "I feel sorry for you, so take this money because it makes me feel good to give, give and give." The rationales for each of these themes are dramatically different. However, both themes finally imply that donors can routinely make donations without receiving counterdonations, and can give help without being concerned with dependency and its ramifications. The succeeding chapter will demonstrate the effects of the spread of these themes through our contemporary society.

What are needed [for the nation] are large-scale efforts that reach the average and below average in natural aptitude or motivation and provide them with the necessary help over a sufficient length of time to make certain their gains are relatively lasting. The [appropriate] environmental supports are: vocational education; employment counselling; job finding; home management instruction; legal services; a wide range of preventive, curative, and rehabilitative health services; adult education of all types; training in the leadership skills necessary for effective and satisfying neighborhood and community participation; and repeated evidence that stability, skill and efforts will be rewarded by an economy that needs and wants full employment of adults....The persons helped will require proof that they are not merely expected to adapt to an unwelcome status quo....

—Winfred Bell[1]

Policy choices for social security can be summed up on two maxims: a little bit of more is a good thing; anything less is inconceivable. There is always forward movement along a familiar, if not actually predestined, path....The result of many steps, each small in itself yet in practice irreversible, is a massive shift of resources to the public sector.

—Martha Derthick[2]

CHAPTER 5

Post-Industrial America

The Great Depression of the late 1920's and early 30's provoked a dramatic shift in the nature of donations to dependent groups. The high level of industrialization and the integration of the American monetary economy existing at that time meant that many of the previous systems of informally enforced reciprocity declined in salience because of the pressures of the depression. Local employers, neighbors, and relatives of the great mass of unemployed persons lacked the resources to offer sufficient donations to sustain them in their desperate need.

The earlier principle of relying largely on informally enforced (i.e., voluntary) donations prevailed for awhile. For example, the American Red Cross, in 1931, rejected a proposed Congressional grant of 25 million dollars to be spent in aiding drought sufferers, and undertook to relieve the sufferers with 5 million dollars from its own disaster reserve and 10 million dollars raised through a special campaign.[3] The efforts to give principal emphasis to informal systems gradually declined as the depression persisted and grew in magnitude. Eventually, increasing recourse was had to county, state, and federal funds collected through formal enforcement processes. In 1929 alone, private contributions for relief in one hundred twenty urban areas averaged 25% of the rate of private contributions during a whole base period, 1931-1933; governmental contributions averaged 13% of governmental contributions for the same period. However, six years later, in 1935, the private contributions were still at 25% of the base period (i.e., they had increased and then declined), while governmental contributions were at 300% of the base period rate (i.e., they had steadily increased).[4] Further, between 1929-1935, governmental contributions in these designated cities totaled 22 million dollars, while private donations totaled 3.7 million dollars.[5] In sum, throughout the period, while the rate of private contributions first equalled the governmental rate, the private rate first rose and then returned to its earlier level, while the governmental rate steadily continued to rise.

One might draw an analogy between the forces stimulating the adoption of the Elizabethan Poor Law in 1601 and the gradual spread of public relief during the depression. The Poor Law — a system relying on formal enforcement — was adopted because the existing systems of informal reciprocity did not seem adequate for the situation; the government relief measures taken during the 1930's were adopted for similar reasons. Of course, the formal systems of the 1930's, like the Poor Law, still gave serious support to the coexisting networks of informally enforced reciprocity. The formal systems were still concerned with principles such as eligibility, settlement, and the obligations of relatives to support one another. However, as we will see, the vitality of many of the principles gradually declined through the operation of the various federal, state, and county welfare laws.

The Creation of Social Security

One group especially affected by the depression was the aged. Employers, in desperate straits, were driven to discharge many older (and marginal) employees whom they probably would have been willing to retain in more prosperous times. Eventually, the many discontented and suffering older persons were attracted to a movement initiated by

Dr. Francis E. Townsend, a physician residing in California.[6] Townsend, in 1933, proposed the federal government pass a highly simplified national pension plan, which would provide all persons over 60 years of age with an immediate pension of $150 a month. His proposal was quite vague as to how the plan would be funded. One authority estimated that the Townsend Movement had about 1.5 million members over 60 years old in 1936. The strident demands of the "Townsendites" were only the culmination of a long process of public agitation directed to winning the passage of some form of federally financed system of old age pensions. These pressures were significantly stimulated by many of the forces already sketched in this book. It should also be recognized that some proponents of the legislation saw such agitation as a device for achieving income redistribution; that is, as a way of using the ballot (i.e., a system of formal enforcement) to require comparatively affluent persons to support those with inadequate means.[7] A final stimulus for support of the legislation undoubtedly came from working persons who felt that such legislation would cause increasing numbers of older persons to retire from the labor market, and thus (supposedly) leave more jobs open to younger workers. Some economists have characterized the theory underlying this argument as the "lump of jobs" approach.[8] This argument implies that there is a limited and inflexible number of jobs, and when someone retires, that job is then made available for another. Conversely, when an older person continues to work he keeps out a younger job seeker.

Eventually, in response to these diverse pressures, the Social Security Act was drafted and passed in 1935.[9] Obviously, the Act created a new formal reciprocal relationship between retired persons and working younger persons.

The general language and popular appreciation of the Act envisaged it as a form of insurance. But this perception was incorrect. Private insurance companies are required to be "funded": to maintain reserve funds, which enable them to pay out all their actuarially calculated future obligations even if all payments from present or future policyholders cease. In contrast, the future level of payments under the Act are dependent on the political judgments of the majority of the voting population at that future time. This is why the "benefits" are really donations.

During the early years of the Act's operations, its potential for intergenerational conflict was muted by a variety of forces. The administrators of the Act, and the legislators prominently identified with its operation, consciously characterized the Act as "akin to insurance." Because of demographic patterns, the number of elderly persons retiring from covered employment was significantly less than the remaining proportion of younger workers in such employment — and so the working young had to assume only modest burdens to assist the retirees. The benefits provided for the elderly at the beginning were not so substantial as they became later through steadily liberalizing amendments.

In any event, regardless of the Act's supposed inviolability, it was frequently amended: from 1935 to 1972, the categories of employment covered were changed 28 times; from 1935 to 1976, the categories of persons provided with benefits changed 53 times; and from 1935 to 1976, the levels of benefits changed 14 times.[10] Of course, nearly all of the changes increased the scope of coverage and the levels of benefits; but what the majority gives, the majority can take away. Nonetheless, supporters of the Act routinely made statements of the following nature:

> The first fact is that payment of benefits are mandated by the law of the land. A claim to social benefits is a legal right enforceable in court.... The second fact is that Congress has gone far — probably as far as any Congress can go in binding its successors — to assure that future legislators will not, by changing the law, weaken the obligation to pay the benefits.... The social security system is, in effect, a compact between the people of the United States and their government. Congress, it is true, retains the legal power to violate this compact, which would be a highly irresponsible act.... If there are doubters among us, they should be reminded that a member of Congress who hopes for reelection will not vote to repudiate a promise to virtually his entire constituency.[11]

Another important element of the Act's retirement provisions conditioned a person's eligibility to receive donations on (1) attaining the age of 65, and (2) refraining from any significant paid employment after applying for benefits. In effect, the Act provided a powerful stimulant for persons to retire at the age of 65. The inhibition on retaining significant employment has at least two important motives: the "lump of jobs" theory already articulated — to make more jobs available for younger workers; and the desire to limit the number of persons receiving benefits — and thus to reduce the costs of the legislation — by excluding from benefits persons over 65 who continue to work.

National Trends Affecting Reciprocity

The Great Depression and its aftermath played a significant role in stimulating the growth of industrial unionism in America. Before the Depression, many workers had belonged to craft unions, but these organizations — perhaps due to their roots in the tradition of individualism — had been comparatively cool to the spread of social legislation such as the Social Security Act. The new industrial unions, however, guided by a more "modern" ideology and based on a membership typically employed in large, industrial institutions, were more sympathetic to using the government as a mediating system to foster remote, formal reciprocity.

World War II saw the further expansion of combined fund raising drives for charities, as such systems were widely applied (on an even larger scale than in World War I) to the solicitation of contributions for war-related purposes. The War also stimulated the adoption of the withholding (or pay-as-you-go) tax by the federal government. That arrangement gradually spread to encompass many units of local government. Most Americans may not realize it, but up until the adoption of the withholding system, taxpayers themselves — throughout each working year — calculated what their annual federal taxes would be, put aside funds to make such payments, and sent the total amount to the government. (Or, of course, people could annually borrow money for the same purpose; but even such an arrangement would require periodic acts of conscious repayment.) The change from deliberate payment to withholding is a classic example of a shift toward an increasingly intangible transaction. From a psychological perspective, one can understand why such intangible transactions might complicate the operation of a reciprocity system or a society.

In the short run, as taxes become more intangible (through withholding), taxpayers may be less sensitive to incremental increases in tax levels, or even to their inherent roles as donors who help pay for civilization. There may even be some illusion that everything donated by the government is "free." Of course, taxpayers will recurrently be reminded this is an illusion. But there is a potential for a form of vacillation between illusion and reality. Conversely, under the earlier, deliberate payment system, taxpayers were regularly and frequently reminded of the direct relationship between the government benefits around them and their personal payments. Such a tangible system may foster a more even-tempered realism in the electorate. If anyone doubts that withholding taxation had the potential for stimulating illusionary approaches in taxpayers, imagine asking any proponent of increased taxation whether he would favor retention of the withholding system over deliberate payments. We assume that proponents of increased taxation inherently tend to favor the withholding system: presumably, they believe that that system does foster illusions in taxpayers.

One might describe the end of World War II as the watershed that marked the appearance of post-industrial society in America.[12] This appearance did not mean the termination of industrial society, any more than the appearance of industrial society in the early nineteenth century marked the termination of agricultural society. Still, that appearance did mean that significantly different modes of production, services, and social interaction were developing in some parts of the culture. These modes were as distinct from the earlier industrial forms as they, themselves, were from their agricultural predecessors. It seems possible that, in an evolutionary sense, post-industrial modes may eventually overwhelm their industrial predecessors, just as industrial and urban modes gradually extinguished their agricultural antecedents, e.g., while about 50% of Americans lived on farms in 1900, only 3.6% did in 1977.

Changes in Intercohort Relations

The characteristics of post-industrial society have important implications for the nature of intercohort exchanges. Some of these characteristics — and their evident implications for intercohort transactions —
can be briefly sketched, while others warrant a more extended treatment.
Affluence is one important characteristic of post-industrial society.
For instance, between 1950 and 1977, median family income in constant (1977) dollars increased from $8,355 to $16,009 per family.[13]
Again, between 1959 and 1977, the proportion of persons living below
an income level defined as poverty (and measured in constant dollars)
declined from 22.4% to 11.6%. The 11.6% figure would be lower
(perhaps near 8%) if various government transfer payments to poverty
families were included in calculating income levels. The affluence has
evinced itself, for our purposes, in the comparative extinction of
necessary household and around-the-house chores for family members;
the widespread availability of efficient, inexpensive transportation; the
increase of housing space and detached housing; the ability of the
society to support younger persons who are not productively employed,
(i.e., who are attending school or are unemployed); and the increased
availability of a variety of medical services. (It should be realized
that this increase in "wealth" is defined in terms of economic affluence: later in this chapter, we will discuss the deficiencies of the
Gross National Product as a measure of necessary or desirable
non-economic services.)

The growth of the suburbs — especially communities where the automobile is an essential means of transportation — is another important
characteristic of post-industrial society. For instance, in 1950, 27%
of all Americans lived within the Standard Metropolitan Statistical
Areas, but outside central cities: such areas could properly be defined as suburbs. By 1977, that figure had increased to 39%, and all
projections assumed its continuing growth. Meanwhile, over the same
years the proportion of the American population living in the central
cities had declined from 35% to 28.4%. The enlarging suburban
environment, for a variety of reasons, provided less intercohort interaction than either central cities or rural environments.[14]

Post-industrial society has also seen the increase in electronic communication and the growth of diverse mass media. The percentage of households with phones went from 62% in 1950 to 95% in 1976, while in 1974, only 3% of all households had no television set, and 45% of all households had two or more sets. These changes in the communication process have lessened the occasions for children and adolescents to collect information or otherwise pass the time engaged in intercohort contacts with proximate persons, or for adults to use children to relay messages to other persons. Of course, the information young people do receive through mass media is ultimately generated by groups of donors (e.g., adult entertainers, directors, and advertisers) who do want to provoke exchanges — they want the young to buy goods. However, these donors have far different motivations underlying their cultivation of youth contacts than other adults traditionally relating to the young. Nor are the adults working in the mass media liable to be effectively monitored by the parents of the young, as proximate community members can be.

Changes in Education Policy

Another characteristic of post-industrial society that warrants more detailed attention is the prolongation and increased bureaucratization of formal education. In 1950, the median number of years of schooling for all persons 25 years old and over was 9; by 1977, the median for these persons had increased to 12.9. The proportion of persons from 25 to 29 years of age with four or more years of college went from 7.7% in 1950 to 24% in 1977. Of course, these increases were only the continuation of a long-term industrial trend toward prolonging and diffusing formal education. Still, the growth reached dramatic levels: between 1950 and 1977, the proportion of the Gross National Product expended on formal education increased from 3.4% to 7.3%, and during the same period, the absolute size of the Gross National Product, in constant 1972 dollars, increased from 53 to 141. These increased expenditures "bought": lower teacher/pupil ratios; more years of education for more pupils; teachers (and college professors) with more years of formal education in their background; and newer and better equipped buildings. The expenditures also assisted the enlargement and bureaucratization of schools, and their further isolation from proximate external communities. Thus, the number of pupils enrolled in the average public high school increased about 140% between 1950 and 1976. Again, between 1942 and 1977, the number of public school districts declined from 108,000 to 15,100, while the total number of pupils served increased 75%. The proportion of children being publicly bussed to school (and thus attending schools outside their immediate community) increased from 27% in 1950 to 55% in 1976. While data about the proportion of teachers covered by collective bargaining agreements are not easily available, it is evident that this figure has greatly increased over the same period.

All of these developments have been reflected in the operation of schools: which practiced increasing intercohort segregation (between different groups of children); in which teachers are increasingly subject-specialists, who present segmented pieces of knowledge to shifting groups of students who come before them for such restricted purposes; and whose formal goal (especially with regards to the more able students) is to prepare students who will make a good showing on college entrance tests. The intercohort segregation usually practiced in these schools differs significantly from the patterns applied in other cultures; as noted earlier, other cultures used such segregation to define group responsibilities for immediate social services (i.e, donations, or counterdonations) to the general society or to other cohorts; in modern schools, age groupings are almost solely used to define the level of curriculum to be presented to students.

Not surprisingly, many observers of such schools have discovered in them an increasing detachment between students and students, students and teachers, and teachers and teachers.[15] In other words, large, bureaucratic institutions, peopled with relatively transitory and docile inhabitants, can be efficient places for accomplishing discrete limited tasks. But they do not stimulate healthy and intense human engagement. The same practices and outcomes have also been observed in many college programs. There are some parallels between these developments affecting the young and the general nature of adult work and life in post-industrial society. However, it is problematic whether the replication and intensification of such patterns in formal education are effective means of socializing the young to live in that adult society. After all, it was realized, in the early stages of the industrial revolution, that putting twelve years olds into factories did not cause them to grow up into effective adults or factory workers; perhaps putting fourteen year olds into schools which duplicate the patterns of emotional life found in a research center or large office is also a questionable practice.

The increase in tax dollars (i.e., formally enforced donations) allocated to formal education might suggest that children and adolescents "have never had it so good." However, such a conclusion would attribute too great a significance to economic, single-purpose donations. Essentially, at an earlier time in American history, a substantial proportion of adult time — the time of parents, relatives, neighbors, older children, and employers — was dedicated to supervising and socializing the young, through participating in exchanges with them. Most of these non-economic and quasi-economic exchanges would not have been computed in the Gross National Product. Today, the sum of these non-economic exchanges (making allowances for population increases, etc.) has declined. This has naturally increased intercohort segregation. The "freed" adult time — to a large degree — has tended to be invested in narrowly economic exchanges, many occurring in paid employment. Thus, I recall a recent newspaper article describing a particular suburban community as being transformed — over a period of about fifteen years — into a daytime desert, as increasing proportions of its mothers left their homes to take full and part-time jobs.

Some of the economic wealth created by this increased paid employment has been tapped via taxes to pay education expenses. But it is extremely unlikely that the "real" per capita value of such formally enforced donations is equal to that of the earlier medley of donations. After all, we are talking about raising human beings, not growing cabbages, treating pneumonia, or winning lawsuits. Healthy human beings are not the product of costly bureaucratic systems, but of engagement, caring, persistent attention, and — most importantly — demanding relationships. In other words, they are the outcome of immediate, continuous, direct, informally enforced exchanges involving persons with greater wisdom and experience. Such exchanges are not created simply by increasing the investment of the Gross National Product in education. Indeed, the higher the Gross National Product goes, the more likely it may be that adults are directing themselves away from serious engagement with the young and into economically defined, single-purpose exchanges.

Segregation Among Cohorts

The intercohort segregation applied in schools has tended to diffuse throughout the entire society. Thus, household size has steadily declined from an average of 4.76 persons in 1900 to 3.52 in 1950 and 2.91 in 1977. This change means that a less diverse pool of persons — relatives, children, servants, boarders — are living within each household. As the size of households has declined, the proportion of persons living alone — i.e., so-called "primary individuals" — has steadily increased. Thus, between 1950 and 1977, the percentage of primary individuals as a proportion of all "household heads" increased from 10.9% to 20.9%. These shifts away from diversity and community — and toward privatization — have been powerfully assisted by economic growth: there are simply more resources available to permit people to afford privacy or, to put it another way, to afford the economic costs associated with avoiding close human contact.

Age segregation has also extended between communities. For example, in 1969, the percentage of persons 65 or over in the Chicago suburban area was 7.5%; but 18% of the population of the suburb of Berwyn was 65 or over, while the figures for the suburbs of Palatine and Bloomington were 4.1% and 3.1%. Furthermore, it is also appearing among states. The South Atlantic and Western states have attracted significant proportions of older persons, while other states have had only slight increases in their aged populations (the outcome of demographic growth plus substantial migration). For example, between 1960 and 1970, the population of persons 65 and older increased 11.3% in Massachusetts, and 78.9% in Florida.[17] This geographic segregation is the outcome of many economic changes. Suburbanization has encouraged the development of relatively homogeneous communities designed for persons with specific life styles and income levels, and which discourage — if not prohibit — residence among them of other types. The mechanization of the household and the growth of pre-schools has made around-the-home help from older relatives less useful. The declining proportion of older persons in the work force (because of retirement) has meant that such persons have less incentive to reside near working environments.

The increase in age segregation has obviously meant a great decline in informally enforced intercohort exchanges that are tangible,

immediate, and continuous. In some ways, such segregation is consonant with certain traditional American philosophic aspirations. Our
society always placed a high premium on independence. The enlargement of wealth has finally made it possible for many of us to afford
to escape, as it were, from intense contact with one another. On
the other hand, in earlier periods of history, while that aspiration
may have been just as vital, the reality of limited means kept it
only an aspiration.

Of course, not all immediate intercohort contacts have been
obliterated — but because people ride on a bus together does not
mean they have become significantly engaged. "Quality" contacts
typically require prolonged interpersonal engagement. Of course, lengthy
contacts may lead to bad outcomes, but brief contacts are more
likely to lead nowhere, except to a sense of unrootedness. Still, the
young and the old are dependent upon the working cohorts. Indeed,
they are probably more dependent than ever before. Thus, there has
been an increase in formally enforced exchanges that are intangible,
remote, and discrete. Some of this increase, in the case of the young,
is reflected in the data already given about education. In the case
of the old, in 1976 about 4.6% of the Gross National Product was
dedicated to federal expenditures financed by social security deductions:
old age survivors insurance, aid for the disabled, and health care of
the aged. Of course, other tax-financed payments (e.g., for food
stamps) also significantly benefit the aged.

The general economic status of the American aged should be
sketched at this point. In 1977, 14.1% of Americans 65 or over were
classified as living in poverty under Census Bureau standards. This
figure represents a significant decline from previous levels for the
aged; for instance, in 1960, the equivalent figure was 35%.[18] The
decline is the outcome of (a) increasing general affluence, (b) raises
in the level of social security payments, and (c) the growth of federal
income transfer programs (e.g., food stamps). Despite these factors,
elderly persons are the American age cohort with the lowest level
of income.

The Growth of the National Government as a Mediator

The increase in the comparative and absolute size of governmentally mediated exchanges in America deserves attention. Between

1950 and 1976, the proportion of the Gross National Product dedicated to non-defense spending (by all levels of government) increased from 21% to 30%. Total government expenses for social welfare, over the same years, increased from 8.9% of the GNP to 20.6% — a 230% increase. In sum, almost all forms of abstract, generalized intergroup dependency (mediated by the government) in our society have been enlarging; at the same time, the appearance of independence has grown. To shift from the general abstract to the concrete, these expenditures are evidenced by the growth of activities and programs such as public schools and colleges, welfare programs, subsidized housing, food stamps, social security, and manpower programs.

Obviously, an enormous variety of forces has provoked this pattern of rising government expenditure. One comparatively novel force should not be underestimated: the government institutions, professional associations, and unions of government workers whose employees and members have developed a vital interest in the enlargement and maintenance of these expenditures. The founders and defenders of the charity organization societies forewarned us of this danger. Our society has attained a point where the welfare of the families of large numbers of competent people (employed by these agencies) is contingent on the persistence of certain forms of dependency. It is simply realistic for us to recognize that this contingency may shape the way many "helping" persons define or handle their work, or interpret social problems to others. Furthermore, many of these same agencies not only distribute donations, but also collect and analyze much of the data on which policy analysis is based. Suppose we discovered that donees might be better assisted by structures that lessened the government donations dedicated to their problems, and that increased the role of immediate, informally enforced donations. What would then happen to the employees of the obsolete mediating agencies?

Another important effect of the growth of governmental mediating agencies has been the evolution of a class of intellectuals who analyze dependency policies but who are not concerned with analyzing *and* significantly participating in the donation process. In other words, there have always been persons who writings have affected our attitudes about donations and mediating systems. In earlier eras, these writers often included persons involved in the practical life of society —

Cicero, Saint Paul, La Rochefoucald, Chalmers, Carnegie — as well as more "removed" theorists. But specialization has generally pervaded society. The scale of formally enforced aid distribution systems has enlarged. A class of intellectuals has evolved who spend much of their time articulating theories about how other peoples' money should be distributed.[19] Many of these intellectuals are academics. Typically, they have neither earned great wealth nor held important responsibilities for making communities work. Thus, their writings are prone to be based on limited — rather than wholistic — perspectives. As a result, the advice available to society about the complex problems of post-industrial reciprocity may actually be of a lower intellectual quality than that proffered in earlier periods.

The Status of The Great Exchange

The many post-industrial changes we have been sketching have also tended to undermine the vitality of the Great Exchange. A key element in maintaining the vitality of that exchange has been the willingness of living cohorts to dedicate time and resources to honoring the achievements of the dead. However, the materialism, individualism, and secularism which pervade post-industrial society cause citizens to regard such acts of veneration as "ritualistic" (in a pejorative sense), uneconomic, and irrational. Hence, efforts are made to escape from the "duty" to the past.

In suburbs, streets are given innocuous and artificial place names (Oak Tree Lane, Shady Drive), instead of being used to remind the residents of their debt to the past. In schools, history is treated as a lightly regarded subject, or as an occasion for the use of revisionism to show children the deficiencies of earlier American leaders. The predetermined dates of holidays honoring past persons and events are moved to insure they coincide with Monday, to permit people to take three day weekends, or they are days on which stores offer special sales. Courts "protect" the rights of students and teachers to refrain from participating in ceremonies honoring the symbols and traditions of the society. Communities are comparatively unwilling — at the most prosperous time in our history — to dedicate resources to the honoring of deceased heroes and achievements. Instead, they designate, as "memorials," utilitarian constructions that would have been built in any event. Even children can recognize the difference between the "messages" transmitted by a road called the "Veterans Memorial Highway," and an elaborate — and "useless" — Memorial Arch. Newspapers frequently — and probably accurately — report that memorial parades attract lessening proportions of marchers. It is evident that the talents of the artists of the society — writers, painters, sculptors, composers, movie directors, and performers — are generally not applied to symbolize and honor the individual and collective feats of generous and self-sacrificing Americans; indeed those talents are more often mobilized to vindicate trivial, materialistic, or egocentric values.[20] Given this unwillingness to venerate the past, it would seem that ambitious people will become increasingly reluctant to commit themselves to long-range, demanding ventures in the interest of the whole society or of important segments of society.

Perhaps these patterns have something to do with the much discussed decline of public leadership; the environment just portrayed provides potential leaders with few incentives to make the sacrifices true leadership usually requires. Of course, someone will always be available to pursue the unoccupied positions set aside for "leaders," but persons of real stature may be reluctant to compete for such unrewarding responsibilities.

It is also significant to recognize that, at the time of this writing, there is widespread intellectual and professional interest in psychological patterns of personal preparation for imminent death. For instance, proposals are being made to provide appropriate surroundings and counsel for the dying. Of course, the immediate events surrounding a persons's approaching death obviously affect his state of "preparation." But it would make more sense to recognize that our deathbed attitudes are largely the outcome of the conduct and values that have shaped our whole lives, especially the factors related to death and the dead. Unfortunately, there is only modest engagement in post-industrial society between the living and the dead: we are prone to deprecate or ignore the contributions of other persons or groups (now dead) to our present welfare. Under these circumstances, dying persons can generally assume that their death will speedily lead to an equivalent obliteration.[21]

Such a prospect may be accepted with resignation. However, it hardly can be gratifying. Naturally, persons whose lives are most deeply embedded in post-industrial society will be among those most profoundly affected by this expectation of extinction. And this anxiety has produced an appropriate response: a society dedicated to bureaucracy, specialization, and rational efficiency has reacted to this psychic challenge by proposing shifts in the institutional arrangements surrounding the dying. Unfortunately, it is probably more necessary to change their own expectations about later remembrance. But those changes will require neither the training and/or employment of new specialists, nor the introduction of new academic courses. Rather, they would require shifts in the day-to-day conduct of most post-industrial adults and youths vis-a-vis honoring the past — since all of us will die and need "preparation." By depriving the dead of honor, we anticipatorily deprecate much of our own lives, and imply that the moment of our deaths will be the time when the living should and will forget about us.

The General Decline of Informal Reciprocity

The above medley of economic and physical changes helped provoke further shifts in public attitudes about exchanges among independent and dependent groups — and those revised attitudes, themselves, have stimulated additional institutional change. One major change vis-a-vis such reciprocity has been the decline of the role of informal reciprocity in the public life of the society. A very diverse group of concepts has appeared as a substitute. From the perspective of dependent donees, these concepts are reflected in terms such as rights, equality, and the broadening of eligibility.[22] The terms suggest that dependent donees have an almost unqualified birthright to donations, and that efforts to compel them to transform donations into reciprocal acts (even through displaying gratitude or deference) are unjustified.

The increased hostility toward reciprocity between independent and dependent groups has been demonstrated in court decisions abolishing the effect of the law of settlement;[23] in statutory and administrative changes diminishing the vitality of the obligation of support among relatives;[24] and in the widespread assumption that students, who are dependent donees, should not be expected to contribute significant amounts of time, money, or energy to improve or maintain the grounds, buildings or operation of the publicly-supported schools and colleges they attend.

In one sense, all of these changes are a logical application of the Pauline concept of charity: we should give without restraint to dependent members of our communities. But the charity of Paul, and that practiced by other religious groups, pertained to small constrained communities or to fellow members of a vital and engaged religion. Communities and religions of such a nature were intolerant of indifference and passivity among their members. They made many implicit demands on dependent groups; thus, they generated a stream of counterdonations from receivers to givers. From the evidence available, it seems that post-industrial society is far less able — or willing — to insist on such counterdonations.

In effect, the concept of charity has been distorted to justify the comparative abandonment of the tradition of reciprocity among dependent and independent groups. This distortion has received much philosophic — or, at least, intellectual — support. First, there is an extensive contemporary literature dedicated to the promotion of strongly egalitarian principles.[25] This literature, both explicitly and implicitly, argues that members of a society or community (in particular, Americans) should receive, by right, a higher level of benefits or economic assistance than they do under their present entitlement. The concept "by right" means that no act of counterdonation (including deference or obvious gratitude) is required in return, and that birth in the community is sufficient to create entitlement.

Second, many psychologists, social workers, and administrators have urged the abolition of laws that establish formal enforcement procedures to maintain intercohort in-family reciprocity. The argument has been that such procedures, or the threat of them, frustrate "warm relations" among relatives. The critics have proposed to make such "tension-creating" obligations the sole responsibility of the state. Thus, one typical review of the statusof aid to the elderly observed that: "In contrast to the spread of government programs for social insurance and public assistance, other legislation, *ironically* enough, places the burden of caring for the indigent old person upon their adult offspring" (italics added).[26]

Third, many economists — of both a conservative and liberal stamp — have conducted extended analyses and assisted in experiments to develop better means of redistributing incomes through increased reliance on formally enforced donations to dependent persons or groups.[27] Many of these analyses treat poverty and intercohort donations as almost solely economic problems. And they thus only concern themselves with the allocation and reallocation of money through formal enforcement systems.

These various contentions hostile to informal reciprocity have focused on poverty issues in general, as compared to intercohort exchanges (but as informed observers, we know the developments have surely affected the operation of schools for the young and programs for the aged). All of them take a far too sanguine and simplistic view of human nature. Clearly, the contentions warrant analysis in terms of their psychological validity.

The Feelings Associated with Reciprocity

The Nobel Prize winning economist Milton Friedman has criticized the current Social Security Act on the grounds that "earlier, the young helped their own parents out of a sense of love and duty. They now contribute to the support of someone else's parents out of compulsion and fear. The *voluntary* transfers strengthened the bonds of the family; the compulsory transfers weaken those bonds" (emphasis added).[28] His discussion is to the point, but it awkwardly intermingles duty, love, and voluntarism, and neglects to say clearly that a sense of duty may well drive us to act under a form of compulsion. It is more helpful to say that both the Act and traditional means of stimulating children to support their parents rely — to significant degrees — on compulsion and volition. The issue is not the meaning of these two vague terms, but the qualitative nature of the reciprocity involved — is it formal or informal?

In another instance, two economists prepared an analysis of a number of income maintenance experiments. In the experiments, groups of workers (and their families) were guaranteed supplementary income for varying periods of years. The aim of the experiments was to see what effects the supplementation would have on work patterns, i.e., how hard would workers seek to earn their living when the "incentive" of deprivation was moderated. The authors, in commenting on the implications of the experiments said "there is little a priori reason to expect the experiment response to be greater than in a permanent program."[29]

A "permanent" program would imply that the citizens of the United States, through their legislators, would adopt a national program of income supplementation on a permanent basis, and put it into large scale operation. The analysts are, in effect, saying that the effects on worker conduct of such a sweeping change would not differ significantly from the conduct of the workers in the experiments. This is ridiculous. The subjects in the experiments live in a country in which the majority of the citizens do not now strongly sympathize with income supplementation programs; if they did, laws creating such programs would be passed. This attitude of the majority of American citizens — including the parents, siblings, and neighbors of the subjects — undoubtedly affect the subjects' conduct during the experiments. Thus, the experiments are highly artificial: it is as if we tested the operation of democracy in the Soviet Union by making one isolated local governing Soviet unit into a "democracy" while the rest of the country remained a totalitarian state. The experiment would be interesting, but it would give us little idea of what would happen — for better or worse — if the entire Soviet society became democratic. The trust seems to be that many "hard-nosed" economists are simply too uncomfortable confronting the complex emotional patterns underlying giving and taking. One is reminded of Chalmers' characterization of the intelligent businessmen who talked in terms of "so many paupers, so many dollars."

Another class of social thinkers and their perspectives can be characterized as "egalitarian." This group seems to have a special fear of frankly "dependent" relationships, i.e., relationships in which donations to a dependent donee are conditioned on gratification being returned to the independent donor. Of course, such gratification — whether it takes the form of goods, overt deference, or gratitude — generates reciprocity. In effect, deference-based relationships recognize that independent donors have power. Somehow, the implicit assumption of egalitarians is that relationships based on such evident dependency are philosophically inappropriate. One writer conceded that the anti-poverty programs had been relatively successful in diminishing poverty. But the programs were still deficient because the donees still had to meet certain eligibility tests. Because of these standards, he maintained, "we have not yet scored a victory over dependency, and reducing dependency is almost as important as reducing poverty."[30] The technique proposed for reducing dependency was a system of guaranteed income regardless of "deservingness."

It is true that the power of independent donors can be exercised to bad ends. However, the persistent focus by egalitarians on the danger of abuse constitutes a sympton of great personal anxiety. All humans — "have nots" as well as "haves" — possess significant potential to abuse power. This pervasive human shortcoming is the reason reciprocity must be *enforced* — either formally or informally. Without such enforcement, the world (or any community in it) would gradually be divided into persons who are essentially only donors or only donees. In contrast, individual members of healthy communities routinely shift back-and-forth between giving and taking. In a non-reciprocal world, independent donors will eventually become extinct, as their resources are exhausted. At that hypothetical moment, some of the donees may realize they have overstretched themselves: no one is creating additional resources to sustain the whole. But it may be too late for donees to change their style. Clearly, the conduct of donees who died before that moment of final assessment was wisely selfish.

Persisting societies and effective donors evolve reciprocity systems that make demands on doness, and they insure, one way or another, that the demands are enforced. Such systems prevent the natural, and perhaps even healthy, tendency toward individual selfishness from overwhelming the commonwealth. Dependent donees who are not well-socialized to reciprocity are naturally prone to resist such demands when they are directed toward them. They may describe the demands as humiliating, debasing, insensitive, and callous. Of course, some requests for reciprocity are inappropriate; but no one should be surprised that human beings may engage in "ingratitude." Debt collection systems exist in all societies because experience has shown that without them, many legitimate debts will not be paid.

Furthermore, if we lower the level of demands for counterdonations made on dependent donees — and such a lowering is the inherent thrust of the pro-egalitarian arguments — there will be less incentive for donors to produce — or to surrender what they have made. Such resistance by donors may engender complex social tension. Under current circumstances, many donees are not conscious of the individual donors whose donations they use and want. Instead, the donees see their donations as coming from "the government," the mediating agency through which the donations of the donors are transmitted. But, as Chalmers observed, when government — in this case, the government of the most wealthy society in human history — stands in the stead of the individual donor, the stimulation of donees' desires will be immense. In other words, an overdose of government-mediated donations is a sure prescription for terrible conflict.

The proponents of "warm family relations" present a slightly different problem. Of course, legal (i.e., formal) enforcement of intra-family reciprocal obligations is cumbersome, and personal relationships have gravely deteriorated by the time such a need arises. However, when the law articulates a legal obligation, it also enhances a social principle. And, where the law fails to maintain a legal obligation, or repeals an existing one, it incidentally deprecates the underlying social principle. The proponents of "warm family relations" at all costs are, in effect, equally critical of both social and legal obligations. But it is impossible to imagine any persisting love-based relationship that does not eventually engender difficult obligations. Relationships without such tensions are relationships without profound love.

Significant, troubling obligations to the aged are inherent in the social process. After all, who will ultimately care for any needy older person but younger working persons — acting individually or col-lectively — who either pay taxes or make direct donations? Does it not seem more psychologically desirable that, whenever possible, the particular younger persons subject to these demands should be those who were nursed, raised, and educated by that older person? Cannot one sense the drama and poignancy that such an exchange adds to human life? This is what is meant by direct reciprocity. Naturally, this poetic desiratum may not always be practical. Still, it is a vision of great emotional value. One might imagine that social planners would try to foster such a vision, to hold it up as an aspiration before both the young and old and, ultimately, to criticize family members who fail to strive to attain such a rewarding but obviously demanding goal. Perhaps the proponents of "warmth" are made uneasy by the fact that attaining this end will not be without obvious costs — as compared to the hidden costs of formal reciprocity systems. Certainly, their reflexive focus on the obvious recalls Chalmers' remark about "lumps of benevolence."

In considering these various shifts in reciprocity systems, we must be careful to avoid simplistic international comparisons. Other countries have welfare and redistribution systems that are different from those in America.[31] Some of those systems provide for more formally enforced donations per citizen than is the case in America. But comparisons between such countries can be unrealistic. America is thirty times as large as West Germany; it has twenty times the population of Sweden; it has only "lived" one-quarter as long as the nation of Great Britain; it lacks the rich symbolic culture of France; it has twenty times as many ethnic minorities as Japan; and, it is a democratic society, unlike the totalitarian regimes in China and the Soviet Union. These differences suggest that the maintenance of informally enforced exchanges in American society may be comparatively difficult, because the proximity, stability, and common values which shape many other societies are less pervasive in America. In other words, the formally enforced welfare systems which are common in many of these other societies may "work" because they are complimented by powerful, informally enforced reciprocity networks. Such networks make it more likely that dependent citizens who use the formal system will have been socialized to reciprocity. For example, the United States Commissioner of Social Security, after a European tour in 1979, reported that he found a greater "solidarity" in Europe between older and younger workers than exists in the United States.[32] In the United States, he observed, each age group has a higher sense of self-interest. But if America begins to adopt too extended a system of formal enforcement — given the current nature of its socialization system — there may not be enough existing informal enforcement in our large, individualistic, heterogeneous society to socialize people to reciprocity.

This discussion about the contemporary disrepute of reciprocity should end with one qualification. Reciprocity is still leading an active secret life in contemporary America. This conclusion is not based on extensive data, but on common sense and everyday observation. Whenever one closely observes effective people working with their associates one can usually recognize that a large proportion of their activities are guided by implicit principles of reciprocity. Such persons do not persistently make significant donations without expecting something in return; and they assume that, by accepting assistance, they create obligations upon themselves. The identification of the acts or goods that constitute donations and counterdonations is not always easy, but careful observers can usually find them. Thus, to put it most simply, when politicians receive valuable favors from special interest groups, the public becomes suspicious: we do not assume those favors are solely intended to be unreciprocated donations. The following anecdote about Chicago city politics in about 1955 is an example of the persistence of such reciprocity:

> I passed this storefront, the 8th Ward Regular Democratic Organization. I went in and said I wanted to help. Dead silence. "Who sent you?" the committeeman said. I said, "Nobody." He said, "We don't want nobody nobody sent." Then he said, "We ain't got no [patronage] jobs." I said, "I don't want a job." He said, "We don't want nobody that don't want a job. Where are you from, anyway?" I said, "I'm a student at the University of Chicago."[32]

Despite the persisting, pervasive secret life of reciprocity, it is probably still correct to conclude that the frequency of immediate exchanges has declined. And it is clearly obvious that the ideological foundations of such transactions have lost some of their validity.

Values and Conduct of the Contemporary Old

What are the attitudes and conduct of old persons living in the contemporary American environment? There is a good deal of data on this question. But the analysis of that data should be tempered with many qualifications. Almost by definition, the data about older persons describe people who have been reared and who have lived much of their lives in rural or industrial societies. Only now, in their old age, are they citizens of a post-industrial society. Therefore, the way these old persons feel and act is not the same way future cohorts of the elderly will feel and act. The data about young persons describe *some* young persons who have lived all their lives in post-industrial environments, and many others (perhaps the majority) who live largely in industrial and sometimes rural environments. Un-- fortunately, much of the data about the young are not broken down in ways that permit us to identify the youths reared in post-industrial environments. Now, after all these qualifications, let us see what we have.

Growing proportions of old persons over 65 are leaving the work force. While in 1900, 68% of males 65 and over were in the labor force, the figure in 1977 had declined to 19.3%. Recent legislative changes — for instance, the federal law severely restricting the compulsory retirement of persons under the age of 70 — may diminish this tendency, but it is difficult to make a clear forecast. Further, some of the egalitarian trends discussed earlier may not be entirely helpful: lowering the wages paid to older and (let us assume) less productive employees is now more cumbersome because of prohibitions against age discrimination.

During this whole period, the labor force participation rates for females 65 and over have remained relatively constant, running between 8-10%. At the same time, the proportions of older persons in the society have steadily increased, from 4.1% persons 65 and older in 1900 to 10.9% in 1977. The proportion of older females in America increased at a much faster rate than did that of males. The proportion of males 65 or over, compared to a constant base of 100 females, has shifted from 102 in 1900 to 68 in 1977. To put it another way, the life expectancy for a female born in 1977 was 76.5 years; for a male, it was 68.7. The shift is due mainly to two health patterns: the death rate of females declined, as a result of medical discoveries, especially those increasing the safety of childbirth; and the death rate of males has not slowed down as much as might be expected, due to the prevalence of tension-related problems (e.g., smoking, obesity, drinking) among males. As a result, growing numbers of females are spending the last years of their lives in widowhood.

The relationships between older persons and their younger relatives are extremely varied. But some general data are available. Table I presents the findings of an international study, dealing with Denmark, Great Britain, and America.[34]

Table I

Nature of older peoples' interaction with children, three countries, 1967

Per cent reporting particular living arrangements and relationships with children

Arrangements and relationships Proximity of children	Older people with living children		
	Denmark	Britain	United States
(1) Children in same household	20.1	41.9	27.6
(2) Nearest child at more than 1 hour's transport distance	12.5	11.0	16.4
(3) Have seen at least 1 child today or yesterday	62.3	69.3	65.0
(4) Have stayed overnight with child within last 12 months	20.0	29.5	42.9
(5) Have had children staying overnight within last 12 months	20.1	26.2	46.0
(6) Those able to do anything for children	27.7	46.9	52.5
(7) Those able to do anything for grandchildren*	13.3	32.8	49.6
(8) Received a regular money allowance within last 12 months	2.5	4.1	4.2
(9) Received occasional money gifts	6.2	20.3	34.9
N =	(2,012)	(1,911	(2,012)

*Percentage computed only for those who have grandchildren. Denmark N = 1719, and United States N = 1873.

Another study, presented in Table II, described patterns of "donations" from older parents in the United States (retired males 69 and over) to their children and vice-versa.[35]

Table II

Congruity of reports by parents and their children
Per cent of parents and children who report each type of contact and aid

Type of contact and aid	Contact and aid given by parents		Contact and aid given by children	
	Reported by parents	Reported by children	Reported by parents	Reported by children
Visit frequently	74	69	74	72
Ask to visit often	74	78	74	81
Write often	53	39	53	29
Take care when ill	51	56	37	46
Give financial help	48	38	10	10
Live close	45	50	46	47
Give advice on business	37	33	30	31
Provide home	9	8	5	8
None of above		3	6	2
N =	(291)	(291)	(291)	(291)

These studies must be treated with many qualifications. They do not show us what the trends are: that is, how old persons were living 30-50 years ago. They deal with particular populations, as compared to large national samples, divided into subsets. And we do not know how representative their populations are. Still, we are probably safe in concluding that the frequency and intensity of proximate transactions between the elderly and the working population have tended to diminish as the result of the many changes in demography and the work force discussed above.[36] This is not to suggest that such exchanges are extinct. There is much research to the contrary. The data in the Tables just presented show there are many contacts. Indeed, some researchers have contended that the current level of intergenerational contacts is satisfactory.[37]

However, some of this "optimistic" research deals with families in relatively "industrial" environments (as compared with post-industrial environments), and some of it deliberately deals with consciously selected samples, e.g., studies of multi-generation families that *have* kept in touch.[38] But neither this research nor the data it has generated provide us with comparisons with the past or dispute the obvious fact that they deal with comparatively restricted (and presumably "decaying") samples.

Many surveys have studied the attitudes of old persons regarding the state of intergenerational isolation (compared to the past) into which they have drifted. These surveys disclose that many older persons are generally satisfied with their current status.[39] They typically say they do not wish greater economic or emotional support from their families, and that they prefer age-segregated communities. But these data must be treated with great caution. Let us recognize what happens in many such surveys. A plausible stranger comes before persons 65 years old or older, and asks them if they would like to have more frequent visits from their children. Assume that the interviewees would like such visits, but know that they are not likely to occur: should we expect the interviewees to confess to the stranger (or even to themselves) that their children — whom they have raised, whom they love, and whose love they still need — are not showing them sufficient affection? That, in effect, they are disappointed with one of the major outcomes of their life? Or, to consider a different example of research, another study discovered that aged persons prefer age-segregated apartment communities when compared to typical, age-heterogeneous urban apartment buildings.[40] However, city apartments are usually regarded as the epitome of impersonality and transiency. Given such a choice, opting for segregation among a group with some sense of self-identity is quite understandable. But findings of this sort might well be interpreted as demonstrating mature resignation — a far cry from the researchers' conclusion that present age-segregation tendencies are inherently desirable for the aged, or that more satisfying (and heterogeneous) options cannot be devised.

Our perspective on attitudes toward age segregation can be broadened by considering the current patterns of age relations in Japan. In 1973, 75% of the persons 50 or older in Japan lived in the households of their children. It is true that there has been a gradual shift toward greater intercohort isolation. Still, in 1972, 52% of persons between the ages of 20-29 hoped to live with their children in their old age. (The lowest proportion of persons wishing such proximity were college graduates, down to 43%.) Furthermore, because of more flexible Japanese work patterns, a larger agricultural economy, and different work attitudes among older persons, high proportions of older Japanese stay in the labor force. In 1965, the participation rate among Japanese males 65 or older was 55%; the comparable American rate was 17%.[41] I do not mean by this presentation to suggest simplistically that America should or can emulate Japan. But it can remind us that attitudes about age segregation are not innate, but learned: that it is difficult to say what are "natural" patterns of intercohort relations. All we can say is that the current American patterns are such-and-such, and then discuss whether they are functional, and (perhaps) how they might be gradually changed.

Can the Young and Old Cooperate?

Researchers, using survey data, have also tried to describe the attitudinal and cognitive differences between the old, middle-aged, and young (as measured by devices such as I.Q. tests and questionnaires). If these differences are substantial, such data might argue for segregating cohorts which possess different capabilities and values.

The studies are partly confounded by the differences in the average length of formal education which exist among American cohorts: essentially, each American cohort has had more prolonged education than its predecessor. And, as other research has demonstrated, such differences in education also cause differences in cognitive ability (as measured by objective, paper-and-pencil tests), and in attitudes. However, this research problem can be moderated if the intercohort comparisons are made between groups of persons with equal levels of education. When such allowances are made, studies of cognitive ability have shown that the scores of older persons on time-structured I.Q. tests tend to decline slightly.[42]

As for measures of attitudinal differences, in 1955 one study analyzed the willingness of respondents — on the basis of responses to attitudinal questionnaires — to tolerate "nonconformists." Such tolerance lessened with age, even when education was held constant: 75% of the college graduates between 30 and 39 years of age were "tolerant," while 31% of those over 60 were so designated.[43] Obviously, the value-laden nature of terms like "tolerance" must be recognized. In other words, "nonconformists" could be drug-pushers, drunken drivers, or profound social critics. The appropriate attitudes to hold toward nonconformist persons is a matter of opinion. It probably is accurate to say that data about such value issues show that older persons, *per se*, are generally less tolerant of deviancy than younger persons. But the optimum level of such tolerance is problematic, and obviously, at some point it can approach destructive indifference.

We do not now know the extent to which intercohort attitudinal differences (which exist even when level of education is "held constant") are the result of (a) being born and raised in different eras or (b) the fact that older cohorts have lived longer — and experienced more — than younger cohorts, or (c) physiological differences among cohorts. To the extent that the differences are due to greater experience, we might be entitled to call them evidence of the wisdom of the aged. After all, it would be grotesque if elderly persons, with a greater number and variety of experiences than younger persons, had the same attitudes as the young. Putting it most baldly, maybe someone learns something important from burying a parent or child; being out of work with a family to support; living long enough so that friends can become truly old friends, or friendships can dissolve; staying married for thirty years or even being divorced; or generally from putting the opinions of youth to the test of events.

All of us have heard of older persons who are admired because they still possess the attitudes typical of the young. It is understandable why such an attribute in the aged is attractive to the young: it implies that the general attitudes of the young are "right" in the long-run; the young-oldsters are a living testament of those attitudes standing the test of experience. However, the more general tendency for human values to shift somewhat with aging may suggest that "youthful attitudes" typically possess some of the transiency generally attributed to the phrase, precisely because adults learn and change even when they are not young. In any case, while there are some real differences between the knowledge and values of the young and old, these differences may just as well argue for increased contacts, which might be to the benefit of both groups. However, such contacts will presumably need more systemic support than that found in a typical urban apartment building.

The role of the aged in politics — especially as active members of pro-aged interest groups — might properly be considered here. It is true that, given the exceptional pressures stimulated by the Great Depression, the Townsend Movement — comprised largely of older persons — was one of a number of forces that brought about the passage of the Social Security Act (though the Act was only remotely related to their specific demands). But, apart from such exceptional occasions, the data reveal that adults, in their older age, tend to follow their earlier patterns of political loyalty.[44] Of course, older adults are interested in age-related issues. However, the data do not reveal the formation of novel age-based personal political identifications, which might stimulate large numbers of older persons to transfer allegiance from one party or cause to another.

The Aged and Retirement

Surveys have studied the attitudes of the aged toward retirement. Essentially, retirement — and attitudes toward retirement — is the sum of a variety of factors. Voluntary early retirement programs in the auto industry have met with considerable worker acceptance[45] (as demonstrated by the persisting gratification displayed by retired workers). But, it is significant that — as I recall from a newspaper story — one union-negotiating demand in that industry some years back was to permit senior workers to "bump" into the position of janitor, with a slight decrease in pay. In other words, the day-to-day life of many production workers is relatively demanding and unsatisfactory. As for more general issues relating to retirement, one survey revealed only 20% of a large sample of retired persons retired solely because they preferred leisure.[46] Other relevant factors (on a check list that permitted one to check one or more items) included "poor health," 43%, "compulsory retirement age," 15%. When the statistical technique called path analysis was applied to these data it revealed that age, *per se,* — whatever that means — was the strongest factor, with a 37% direct effect for males.

Retirement provoked by poor health should be viewed with some perspective. Health does decline as one grows older: 85% of persons 65 or older suffer from one or more chronic conditions.[47] But this decline is highly incremental. For instance, 66% of the American middle-age population under 65 also report one or more chronic illnesses. As for serious disabilities, only 8% of persons 65 or older are confined to their homes or institutions as a result of disabilities. In sum, human decline is often quite gradual and its tempo varies greatly among individuals. Unfortunately, a growing proportion of employers are unable to restructure imaginatively the jobs held by older workers (including measures such as lowering salary rates) or to make distinctions among older workers on criteria apart from chronological age.

The efficient bureaucratic procedures of post-industrial society — which insure easy determination of the chronological age of almost all workers — actually handicap institutional adaptability. If we did not have such records — as was typically the case 100 years ago — retirement decisions in industry would have to be based solely on the observed capability of workers. But modern recordkeeping has helped destroy such individualization.

There are other forces shaping retirement policies. Younger persons employed alongside older workers today have few incentives to help restructure work so as to retain older workers — as compared to family members on a farm, who are directly responsible for maintaining the older family members whom they choose to "pressure" out of farm work.[48] In modern work, the economic costs of maintaining retired persons are typically borne by some large impersonal entity: General Motors, the garment industry pension fund, or the U.S. government. These abstract burdens on all workers are just as real as the extra tasks assumed by family farm members, but they are so widely dispersed that there is not dramatic incentive for the persons responsible for the retirement of others to engage in some form of adaptation.

In any event, middle-aged persons in modern society, for perhaps twenty years before they attain 65, have before them a relatively clear picture of the mechanics of their prospective exit from employment. For many workers, there are few late-in-life jobs issues for them to negotiate; by that time most issues are determined by factors beyond their personal control. Under these circumstances, it is not surprising that "poor health" and "age" are frequently given as retirement "causes," since most modern work environments are unable to engage in even modest adaptations to the talents of older workers. Furthermore, many older workers may be wise to be reluctant to continue working when no adaptations are made to their changing needs. Retirement is obviously better than that. The economic costs of this non-adaptation are pushed off on the total society. And retirees, as mature persons, accept the inevitable.

Another factor allegedly shaping retirement policies should also be discussed. It is often contended that older workers lack the extended formal education of most younger workers, and thus are unable to contribute satisfactorily to production. As already noted, older workers generally do not have as much formal education as younger cohorts. However, the exact relevance of such knowledge is highly problematic. There is little or no definite information as to the relationship between most school-type knowledge and work proficiency — beyond some obvious generalizations relating to literacy and the like. One careful study of the relationship of education to on-the-job-learning among the college-trained engineers employed by a large manufacturing organization disclosed that only 20-30% of their work required formal academic training. The bulk of their work (70-80%) was based on job-learned skills.[49] Some informed persons have contended that educational criteria are frequently used as very rough screening devices when the labor market is loose; as it becomes tighter, decisions are made on increasingly relevant criteria.

The "lump of jobs" theory (i.e., to retire older workers and make way for younger ones) was one of the underlying reasons for the passage of the Social Security Act. That theory has been generally discredited among economists, although it still has a wide popular appeal.[50] The theory confuses micro- and macro-economics.

In a microeconomic sense, imagine a hypothetical worker whose immediate superior is about to retire. When the superior retires, the worker is promoted; there may even be a series of promotions all along the line, perhaps even traceable down to the new employee who is hired at the bottom. However, the dependent retired worker does not go off and die; he is fed, housed, and generally maintained through remote, indirect donations. Workers throughout America must produce and donate the goods he uses. The donations can be enforced by different means: social security deductions, payments of pension premiums, or family members helping one another. And, because the dependent donee is retired, he cannot easily reciprocate those donations. Thus, in a macroeconomic sense, there are many working-age "losers" everytime someone who is capable of working retires. Indeed, from the general viewpoint of the working-age population, the most efficient rule would be to compel older people to continue working until they can no longer stand (and, apparently, that is what happens on farms, where the costs of retirement to the sur-viving workers are highly immediate).

Another economic factor in retirement decisions is the effect of funded pension plans, such as those maintained by many employers (frequently as a result of collective bargaining). These plans set their rates of contribution as if all covered employees will retire at a pre-determined retirement age. There is a peculiar structural effect to many of these plans. As an employee approaches retirement, *if* he chooses to ignore the typical retirement age, he would continue working, *even though* his earlier pension deductions were computed as if he would retire on schedule. In other words, his earlier deductions were higher than necessary. And, under many pension plans, if his deductions were more than his needs, he does not get them back; they are simply paid over to other employees who retire on schedule, and who consequently need more pension income than do continuing workers. In this way, may pension structures penalize older em-ployees who choose to continue to work and favor employees who choose to stop being productive in the work force.

Attitudes and Conduct of the Young

There is a significant amount of data about the attitudes and conduct of the young in post-industrial society. Because many of the data have already been recited elsewhere by the author, they are summarized in the Appendix. The data make it clear that young persons are feeling increasingly detached from society and somewhat desirous of maintaining and intensifying that detachment. They also see society as increasingly less cooperative and supportive, although society has dedicated a growing proportion of its Gross National Product to assist them. Finally, anti-social acts and destructive conduct by the young have steadily increased over relatively long periods of time (15-25 years).

The level of youth employment (one form of intercohort exchange) has remained comparatively stable over the past ten to twenty years, although this level is significantly lower than it was in previous periods. Other than information about employment, there are no significant data available about the quantity or quality of immediate intercohort exchanges affecting the young. However, as suggested earlier, there is ample evidence implying that tangible, immediate intercohort exchanges involving the young have steadily declined. In place of such exchanges, the independent adult society has tended to donate: formal education; suburban security financed by post-industrial affluence; the child-care services of television, radio, record players, and diverse toys; and the subsidized free time of child and adolescent peer groups. These donations have evident economic and emotional costs to adults. But many of these costs are intangible, remote, and indirect. During their dependency, young persons in post-industrial society are not expected to engage in significant counter-donations (or acts of reciprocity) in exchange for these adult donations. Perhaps their obligation to learn and wait while attending school can be treated as an immediate counterdonation, but that donation is highly intangible and indirect. It is not surprising that many young persons find that the status of studenthood is pervaded with dependency: their counterdonation (i.e., their learning) may just not be tangible enough to give them a sense of reciprocity — or control — vis-a-vis their donors.

The Social and Economic Contributions of Females

The additional economic costs to the society generated by the increase in retired persons (i.e., dependent donees) have been met in part by the enlargement of the size of the national labor force. This is so even though there are fewer older workers and no increases in the proportion of young workers. The labor force englargement is due to the increasing proportion of female workers. Here are the key data. In 1960, 60.2% of all persons 16 or over were in the labor force; by 1978, the size of the force had increased slightly to 63.7%, even though the rate of male participation had declined from 82.6% to 78%. But, over the same years, the rate of female participation had gone from 36% to 47.4%. In other words, the total value of the output of the American labor force has increased because new classes of workers developed as other groups became less available. But there is undoubtedly some ceiling to the potential level of rising female employment. And the proportion of dependent retired workers is certain to enlarge.

I do not mean to suggest here that the female increase represents a change in the "activity rate" of females; presumably, it simply signifies a shift from economically uncompensated to economically compensated activities. Or, to put it another way, a shift from informal to formally enforced exchanges. Incidentally, we are sometimes told that one major cause for the shift is economic need: families "need" two incomes in order to live. However, the issue of "need" is highly subjective. Between 1960 and 1977, the real income of American families greatly increased. Thus, if most females gradually stopped working, perhaps the worst thing that might happen is that we would go back to living at our 1960 income level. In other words, when we say we "need" a certain income, we mean we need it to maintain a level of life we view as desirable. First we have expectations, and then "needs." And, human expectations are infinitely expansible. Thus, modern "needs" often include orthodonture, foreign travel, psychiatric treatment, a comparatively high level of family privacy, college for the children, or air conditioning in the home. If we could learn to call such needs "desires," we might treat them more realistically.

Restatement

We have just considered a macrocosmic sketch of shifting patterns of exchanges among dependent and independent groups, and among cohorts in particular. Beyond this general analysis, we do not have a precise idea of what is — or was — going on among the millions of human beings engaged in this immense social transformation. Still, from the macrocosmic data and our other information, it is evident that the frequency and quality of contacts among these various groups has declined. At the same time, the amount and proportion of money donated (as compared to other forms of help) has increased. But what we may have is people giving — and receiving — more and enjoying it less.

In describing the situation, we can apply a new term, "pure dependency": the dependency that arises when donees make no counterdonations of any form. The level of pure dependency in our society is probably at an historical high. It is reflected in the focus on the rights of donees, in the parasitic nature of most modern studenthood, and in the increasing isolation of the aged from social and work life. The exact psychic effects of pure dependency are difficult to identify at this point. Still, there are signs that the attenuation and extinction of reciprocity do generate complex psychic dissatisfactions; e.g., perhaps they were a partial cause of the student unrest of the late 1960's and early 1970's.

The social and demographic data suggest that the level of dependency by the aged will continue to increase. The continuation of our current policies will tend to translate this dependency into pure dependency, which, in turn may eventually be the cause of future problems for the contemporary cohorts of the young and middle-aged. If we want to prevent this contingency, we must direct our attention toward the socialization systems now surrounding our young. Those systems should be changed in order to change the attitudes the young are now acquiring. To bring about such changes, the middle-aged must reform their own conduct and expectations.

In other words, I am contending that the currently controlling cohorts are now determing the values of the youth who will grow to share political power with them, and who will ultimately decide the future policies toward the aged. The young and the middle-aged are making their own future through the socialization systems they are now maintaining.

Early reformations are amicable arrangements with a friend in power; late reformations are terms imposed upon a conquered enemy: early reformations are made in cool blood; late reformations are made under a state of inflammation. In that state of things the people...never attempt to correct or regulate: they abate the nuisance, they pull down the house.

—Edmund Burke[1]

CHAPTER 6

Forecasting, Analyzing, and Prescribing

To maintain textual coherence, this chapter will focus almost entirely on issues relating to intercohort exchanges. Much of the preceding material extended beyond this issue and discussed exchanges among all independent and dependent groups. While some of the material discussed in this chapter has ramifications beyond the issue of intercohort exchanges, those ramifications are either ignored or treated summarily.

Some developments structuring the future of intercohort exchanges in America are susceptible to relatively precise forecasts. Other developments are more problematic. But, ultimately, the pattern of such exchanges will be the outcome of the interaction between both the more and the less foreseeable developments. Some of the more problematic developments are uncertain because they are susceptible to deliberate manipulation in both the present and the future. Thus, they may be worthy of the greatest attention. In any case, a useful forecast — one which will assist us in shaping the future of our society and the character of our lives — must deal with both foreseeable and problematic future developments.

Demographic Forecasts

Demographic projects are one type of comparatively foreseeable development. They can help us forecast the absolute and proportionate size of different American age cohorts. Because the death rate for older persons has been declining in a slow and incremental fashion, we can make comparatively accurate forecasts of the absolute number of persons 65 or older who will be alive at specified future dates. Thus, in the year 2,000, there will be approximately 31.8 million such persons alive in America; in 1977, the figure was 23.4 million.[2]

The more complex demographic question is the proportion of such old persons compared to other age cohorts. This statistic can be affected by future birth rates; thus, it cannot be forecast with precision. Still, the comparative and absolute size of different age cohorts now alive provides demographic parameters which establish minimum and maximum ranges for population change forecasts. For example, if the cohort born between 1970 and 1980 is comparatively small, the number of babies born when this cohort reaches child-rearing age will be similarly constrained, even if we cannot forecast the average family size for that future date. The Bureau of the Census has developed alternative projections of American population change. The character of the various national demographic profiles presented by these forecasts is suggested by the different national median ages derived from the profiles. In 1977, the median age of our population was 29.4 years. The median age of the American population in the year 2000 based on the Census alternative projections, termed I, II, and III, would be 32.5, 35.5, or 37.3 years. A fourth Census projection, based on the assumption that America is at zero population growth by the middle of the twenty-first century, would provide a median age of 36 in 2000.

These forecasts about cohort size permit us to derive projections about potential "dependency ratios." The dependency ratio is the proportion of persons above or below working (i.e., productive) age compared to the proportion of working age persons. The denominator of the ratio is the working population, while the dependents comprise the numerator.[3] Certain assumptions, beyond matters of demography, underlie such projects: that few adults over 65 will be productively employed, and that some specified age (e.g., 18 years) is a realistic point at which to consider a person a productive adult. Later in this chapter, we will discuss these assumptions further. In any event, the following data present the current and some projected dependency ratios. The projections are based on Census projections I and III.

U.S. Dependency Ratios for Persons Under Age 18, and Age 65 or Over
(Based on specified assumptions)

1977	2000	2050
67.6	67.4*	73.1***
	56.7**	

*Based on the Census projection I, which assumes a national median age of 32.5 in 2000; the 1970 median age was 29.4.

**Based on the Census projection III, which assumes a national median age of 37.3 in 2000.

***Based on Census projection which assumes America will attain zero population growth in the mid-twenty-first century.

Some of these future dependency ratios do not vary greatly from the current ratios. However, the underlying groupings of age cohorts do significantly change. Essentially, the proportion of dependent youths will decline, and the proportion of dependent oldsters will increase. These changing proportions are described in the following data:

Persons Age 65 or Over, as a Proportion
of Present and Future Dependent Cohorts
(Based on specified assumptions)

1977	2000	2050
26.8%	23.3%*	43.8%***
	35.9%**	

*Based on the Census projection I.

**Based on the Census projection III.

***Based on the Census projection which assumes America attains zero population in the mid-twenty first century.

The Costs of Dependent Cohorts

One might naturally wonder whether an elderly dependent or a young dependent is more costly. The data on this important issue are obscure. Probably it is more costly to maintain a dependent adult than a child. The adult might want a car, private or semi-detached housing, and other conveniences. Also, his medical costs will steadily increase with age. On the other hand, we should not ignore the costs (to parents and society as a whole) of providing children with extended formal education, as well as basic necessities. Obviously, it would be useful to have more precise estimates of the cost effects of these patterns of dependency. Such estimates will be founded on important (and often implicit) assumptions.

There is no final definition of how much a good education should cost, or how long people should attend formal education. And there is also no final definition of how much personal and medical care should be made available to the aged. The amount and quality of care that can be used by both the young and the old (but especially the old) are almost infinitely expansible. And we can be sure that new discoveries will arise to change the nature (and probably the costs) of care of the aged. We should also recognize an important psychological difference between the "emotional" costs of providing help for the young, as compared to the old.

Working age cohorts have an evident need to support the young: their own security in old age is dependent on the maturation of those cohorts. Furthermore, the counterdonations of the young to society still lie ahead. One can easily have optimistic imaginings about how these donations will redound to the benefit of the donees who helped the young. However, the donations of the aged, on the whole, are irrevocably determined. If working age cohorts choose to ignore or undervalue those donations — or if they rationally conclude that the aged, in the prime of their life, did not act in a manner that now entitles them to significant donations — little or no "retribution" can be visited on the workers who make such a collective decision. Thus, the foreseeable shift in the composition of our dependent cohorts presages the evolution of new intercohort tensions in the society.

Historically, intercohort dependency costs were almost never borne only by the nuclear family. The nuclear family is too narrow a social unit to provide children and adolescents with sufficient learning experiences to make them competent adults. Because society had too great a stake in the outcome of childrearing in individual families to leave complete authority (or responsibility) in that unit, other social groups had to make some of the inevitable donations associated with such socialization. In the case of the aged and infirm, the potential burden that might be generated for a nuclear family by an elderly adult could be immense. But that adult, during his active life, had the opportunity to develop a network of descendants and friends. These circumstances meant that the individual family might expect donations from others in aiding its own elderly. As this text has emphasized, all of these donations, whether micro- or macroeconomic, or comprised of dollars, or love and time, should be treated as intercohort exchanges — although the transactions take different forms. The demographic data presented above clearly imply that individual nuclear families and other small communities will be faced with stresses that mirror the increasing intercohort tensions in the larger society.

The Costs of the Young

We have macroeconomic data about some of the past and present economic costs of intercohort support systems. In 1950, formal education absorbed 3.4% of the American Gross National Product; in 1977, the comparable figure was 7.3%. Most of these expenditures were donated to help young persons, though many of the donees were over 18. The considerable increase in costs was caused by (a) the steady prolongation of school, and college attendance by students; (b) an enlargement in the size of the youth cohort (in 1950, 31% of the population was under 18; in 1960, the figure was 35.8%); and (c) the growth of pre-school programs. As to this last factor, between 1965 and 1977, the proportion of the successive cohorts of children aged 3-5 enrolled in such programs increased from 27.1% to 49.5%. Most of these children were undoubtedly enrolled in part-of-the-day programs, or only two or three days a week, as compared to five day, all-day programs. Still, the care of young children is demanding; a reasonable quality full-day, full-week program might cost $3,500-4,000 per child per year. Thus, the costs of this increase have been substantial.

As for the future cost level of formal education, it is unlikely that the costs of elementary, secondary, or higher education, as a proportion of the Gross National Product, will continue to grow. The proportion of the young who choose to become college students may continue to fluctuate slightly, but youth cohorts will inevitably decline as a proportion of the total population. It is possible that pre-school costs may increase. The growth rate for such pre-school costs can be affected by increases in the (a) proportion of the cohort enrolled, (b) the length of time per day or week or year children spend in school, or (c) the "quality" of care provided, through an increase in either the ratio of staff to children or length of staff training.

Theoretically, one might speculate we could significantly decrease the proportion of our GNP dedicated to formal education and spend the money saved on older people. After all, assume that a small community or family discovered that its proportion of aged persons was enlarging, and its proportion of young persons declining. We would simply expect the group members to devote more of their time to helping the aged rather than the young. The total amount of helping would not necessarily increase — just its nature. But once a society relies on large mediating systems and formal donation processes, compared to informal reciprocity systems, many rigidities make their appearance. As a first step in forecasting changes affecting donations to the young, let us analyze the arguments for holding back educational investment.

At a purely economic level, America expends a far higher proportion of its GNP on formal education than any other major industrial country. Despite such expenditures, between 1950 and 1976, America had the lowest average rate of economic growth of the seven major democratic industrial states.[4] One cannot simply infer that extending our investment in education has "caused" this drag in the growth of our GNP. However, the economic benefits of education to the whole society have been an important argument advanced to justify heavy investment in education. The data just recited are apparently inconsistent with that proposition. And there obviously must be some point at which enlarging investment in education can become uneconomic. Just because education was a "wise" investment for the society in 1950 or 1910 — when we increased the proportion of elementary school or high school graduates — does not automatically mean it is socially efficient for working adults to make substantial sacrifices to create a society comprised of 30% to 50% college graduates.[5]

Of course, we may want to disregard economic costs — and economic benefits — as appropriate tests of education efficiency. We may simply argue that America invests in education because educated people are good for the country. And, therefore, we should continue — or even enlarge — our donations to education. But we should probably be more precise about the concept of "good for the country." To a significant degree, working age cohorts donate resources to maintain costly socialization systems (such as education) because of "selfish" motives. They want such systems to produce adults who will, in the future, (a) cooperate — as workers, parents, neighbors, and citizens — with the current adults to help the society, (b) provide security to the current adults when they attain old age, and (c) reverently recall and memorialize the achievements of previous living and dead cohorts.

These aspirations may seem harsh or to many American ears: we rarely put things so bluntly — or frankly. Perhaps it is just too difficult for working age Americans to admit that they do and will depend on the current cohorts of the young — such overt dependence seems un-American. But with some simple rephrasing, we may recognize the general applicability of the preceding proposition. Consider terms such as "expectations" or "aspirations" for our young. Or recall phrases about the young representing "our future."

These terms are popularly used to characterize many of our motives for educational expenditures. They suggest that working age cohorts have aspirations for their future and are making donations to help younger cohorts attain those goals. Assume these adult cohorts were told that their expectations were unrealistic, that their aspirations were foolish, and that "their future" would be ridden with frustration, pain, and poverty because of the conduct of younger cohorts. Does any reader doubt that such a revelation — if it could break through the inevitable and natural tendency toward denial — would have a shattering effect on popular attitudes toward education? Indeed, what image of human beings would one have, if one imagined working age adults who choose to bear and rear children and support education taxes expecting that such children will ultimately deny the values and achievements of their parents and providers, and refuse them decent support in their old age? Surely, such masochism is too grotesque to be plausible.

Suppose we can accept the prevalence of "selfish" and "healthy" motives among working age cohorts for the support of education. Then there is evidence — already mentioned, and sketched in the Appendix — that successive youth cohorts have contained increasing proportions of drug users, alcohol users, procreators and bearers of illegitimate children, and of persons generally prone to hedonistic, self-destructive, and other-destructive conduct. These increases have occurred over the same years that our investment in formal education increased to its historic high. Do these data give one a sense that we are rearing dependable cohorts? Is it realistic to assume that such youths will automatically mature into adults who will provide the counterdonations expected by their predecessors? And, if such expectations are unrealistic, is it not likely that working age adults will cut back their donations for formal education?

Despite the "logic" of cutting public budgets supporting formal education, especially extended education, there are many elements resisting such cuts. We must recognize that we are talking about tax-supported enterprises. Such systems of remote, indirect, formally enforced donation stimulate parents of school age children and college age youth to encourage increased public support for formal education. After all, at small personal costs, they can get some benefits out of tax-subsidized education; on the other hand, if these same persons had to pay their own — or their children's — total education costs, they might well decide that as the system is now run, it is not "worth" it. And so, it has become reasonable for users to encourage the continuation of an "inefficient" tax-supported education system as compared to spending their own money to support one that is more efficient. This dysfunctional effect is a logical outcome of any system of intercohort exchanges that relies on excessively remote exchanges: individual users are tempted to free-load or to increase the availability of non-reciprocated, poorly managed donations. Theoretically, such "inefficiencies" should be corrected by the general political process and the foreseeable resistance of taxpayers to counterproductive donations. But taxpayers are a diffuse group, whose strategies are ridden by conflicting aspirations; in contrast, formal education and its public allies have limited aims — survival and the growth of the institutional *status quo* — and many institutional resources.

Improving Socialization

The current level of investment in formal education is also "protected" by the paucity of effective socializing alternatives for the young in the society. America has moved toward a point where many of the agencies that traditionally helped to socialize our youth and children — homes, families, neighborhoods, jobs, farms, churches — have greatly declined in vitality. Of course, many of these agencies still "exist." However, the particular characteristics that helped them to be effective socializing forces have steadily been drained away: there are fewer chores around the home; families are often portrayed principally as vehicles for adult personal self-development or sexual expression, and the divorce rate is steadily climbing; and suburban neighborhoods frequently are composed of detached homes, whose inhabitants have only occasional and casual contacts.[6] If we want to lower our investment in formal education, it will be necessary to stimulate the gradual revival and restructuring of these agencies to permit them to resume their traditional roles. Or, alternatively, we could commit resources — not necessarily money, but surely time — to creating new, effective, socializing systems. Such creation, if it were effective, would have to occur incrementally. Still, it would eventually have enormous costs: large numbers of people would have to reorganize the way they spend their time — in effect, to change the way they live, so as to maintain different forms of adult-youth relations throughout the society. In any event, developing socializing systems to partially replace formal education would produce many new emotional demands on Americans, in their jobs, homes, and communities. We may feel that paying taxes for comparatively inefficient schools is cheaper than confronting such demands.

It is also possible that expenditures for formal education might be made more "productive." Then the existing level of costs would become less of a burden on working age cohorts. Such a development would require us to restructure substantially many of our existing systems of formal education. Conceptually, there is nothing impossible about this objective. A large number of different types of formal education have existed throughout American and world history.[7] Even in contemporary America, there is considerable variety among schools. Unfortunately, despite this variety, many of the larger schools and colleges are precisely those which tend most to undermine intercohort reciprocity. Thus (to offer some arbitrary but illustrative figures), perhaps 40% of the schools and colleges are "constructive"; but that virtuous 40% enrolls only 15-20% of the total number of students. Further, the country's more potentially talented youth are more likely to be enrolled in "destructive" schools (if, for the moment, we define potential only in terms of I.Q. scores). The destructive schools follow policies that: rely heavily on trained professionals and specialists; encourage economies of scale; focus on cognitive learning rather than learning that inculcates wholesome, pro-social attitudes; and emphasize individualism rather than cooperative values.

We could easily conceptualize schools with different aims and outcomes than those in general favor at this time. Or, indeed, we could even try to identify and replicate the schools that are following "constructive" policies. Unfortunately, a great deal of economic and human capital is invested in the destructive *status quo.* Campuses have been designed and buildings constructed. Millions of educational employees have made career commitments, undergone training, been hired, and acquired seniority and tenure. These steps have all been taken on the assumption our current modes of operation will continue. Any substantial change in these modes will be costly and stressful because of the rigidity created by such previous investments. But a more significant barrier to change is the public's emotional investment in the educational *status quo.*

As has been already suggested, this emotional investment is partly philosophic. It is founded on certain views of the nature of human relations. Thus, it is generally considered bad form, in post-industrial society, to suggest explicitly that children, when they mature, owe serious, continuing obligations to their parents and to the society that has donated so many benefits to them. As noted, such propositions — about the "debt" of the young to the older cohorts — are actually implicitly accepted by most persons. But there is a great difference between *implicit* and *explicit* acceptance. To socialize the young to appropriate reciprocity, one must establish relatively clear standards, present attractive role models, and surround them with powerful and dramatic systems of reinforcement. Such arrangements are not feasible unless we are committed to "telling" the young that we expect to be "paid back," that "repayment" is honorable, that "parasitism" is despicable, and to making pro-reciprocity values the norm in school.

Adult Ambivalence About Reciprocity

Another attitudinal problem is our basic American ambivalence about explicitly recognizing dependency. While various forms of macro-economic dependency — by both the young and old on working age cohorts — pervade the society, such donations are rarely portrayed to their donees as donations — acts of generosity, love, and gratitude. And so, when the young become taxpayers, they rarely see the reality of the indirect exchange they are helping to repay. Furthermore, we have already noted that immediate, continuous, informally enforced reciprocity is still a vital part of the secret lives of most effective adults. But such covert patterns are of little help to the young. Indeed, such adult practices probably increase the confusion of the young, as they gradually — in late adolescence — become aware of this secret norm, are shocked, and grumble about cronyism and manipulation.

(In a recent magazine piece, I saw a reference to Tom Wolfe's characterization of the media as "The Victorian Gentlemen." He was referring to the media's propensity for expressing intense indignation at discovering that some politician had recognized a reciprocal obligation: "He made a deal!" Wolfe implied such indignation was hypocritical — in someone running a substantial business operation — or unbelievably stupid. His point is well taken, though it may be a little hard on the Victorians. Unfortunately, I fear too many students and school teachers have failed to attain Wolfe's sophistication. As for college faculty, if they do not know the practice of reciprocity, I do not see how they attained tenure. However, we still tend to treat the practice of reciprocity as a dirty secret.)

In sum, a major reason for the decline in the efficiency of schools as institutions for socializing the young to reciprocity has been the unwillingness of most of the adult population to defend frankly and persuasively the essential humanity of reciprocity: to remind us that it also represents fellowship, and is a vital means of tempering the pervasive selfish instincts that abound in mankind. This adult unwillingness evinces itself in two patterns of thought that have already been portrayed. One pattern implicitly says, "So many students, so many dollars; insure they learn cognitive knowledge, and leave them to find their way."[8] The other says, "Give the young personal attention, encouragement, and love, and ask for nothing in return. Things will work out for the best."

These patterns are congruent with the two flawed systems of donation recognized and powerfully criticized by Chalmers in Edinburgh. One pattern leads to distance between most adults and the young, and the other encourages contact. However, both substitute donations for intercohort exchanges and engagements, and both fail to recognize the need for intimate support *and* demands, for concern with shaping both thought and feelings. This adult ambivalence has had its effect on school policies. Our schools have been increasingly unwilling and unable to articulate philosophies that tend to bind cohorts together both within and without their walls. And unbound people are naturally prone to alienated conduct. If we hope to improve the outcome from our vast investment in both formal education and the general socialization of our young, we must frankly articulate and effectively defend the role of reciprocity in maintaining human society. Such an effective defense should not rest on presenting the young with details of a deep or complex philosophy. Instead, it should rely on the purposeful manipulation of symbols, the deliberate and skillful management of intercohort relations, and the humane but firm determination to practice successful indoctrination. In other words, we must be commited to produce more fellowship among students and adults, just as we are now committed to generate literacy or regular student attendance at classes.

Future Donations to the Aged

Our future donations to the aged will be similarly shaped by a combination of precise and imprecise factors. In 1976, the Old Age, Survivors Insurance, and Disability Insurance Programs (which essentially comprise the retirement provision of the Social Security Act) absorbed 5.2% of our Gross National Product. The tax rate for the program in 1980 was 12.26% of eligible incomes. Legislation has been passed providing for higher rates in the future, but it is uncertain that the raised rates will be put into effect because they can be reversed (before their operative date) by legislative amendments.

The electorate will be subject to a variety of pressures to increase the tax rates and to maintain any higher rate already passed so as to raise the level of benefits to the aged. One such pressure will be the rising dependency ratio for the aged. Other sources of pressure may be economic growth: if there is such growth, and the polity wishes to maintain the aged in a status proportionate to that of younger cohorts, then the tax rate must be increased.

One typical projection of Social Security tax rate increases used Census projection II and several other median assumptions about economic developments.[8] Under this projection, by 2000, the tax rate on eligible incomes should rise to 16.2% — a 32% increase over 1980. By 2025, the rate should be at 23.8% — a 91% increase. Of course, these calculations ignore the many other donations for care of the aged that come through the food stamp program, various pension and welfare systems, voluntary service organizations, and relatives. If this elaborate network of donations does not satisfy the needs of the aged, there will be growing pressures for other types of help. Whoever nominally donates such help, it ultimately will come from the pocket of "society."

Like donations for formal education, future levels of donations to the aged are affected by numerous problematic assumptions (and attitudes). One assumption is that steadily increasing proportions of aged persons will retire at 65. But this retirement pattern is the product of social forces that may be subject to manipulation. These forces include the current attitudes of late middle-aged people (potential retirees), and their co-workers and employers; the salary and job structures employers maintain; and the formulas applied in determing whole or partial eligibility for social security and retirement benefits.

Another relevant assumption is that the current modes of residential and geographic age segregation will persist and spread. This segregation may be a rational response to the impersonality that pervades many current age-heterogeneous residential environments. However, that segregation increases the pressures on the elderly to retire from work so they may move to segregated living environments. It also lessens the possiblity of improving contacts between the young and the old. But once again, the assumption of segregation is subject to manipulation through various devices.

A final pertinent assumption is that there are few roles for the elderly other than paid employment or "pure dependency." Of course, this is incorrect. Many important social contributions — child care, different forms of teaching, social services — can be made by uncompensated workers. Or, to put it another way, much can be done by workers who are not paid in dollars, but with respect and consideration. It is true that such donations by volunteers are not included in computing the Gross National Product. However, they usually add to the true sum of national wealth. And a disproportionate increase in such donations — as a result of changing patterns of conduct by the aged — might significantly lessen the true costs of our rising dependency ratio.

At this time, it is unlikely that the large proportions of the cohorts about to retire will select many of the cost-reducing options just presented, for their options are constrained by personal and general expectations, as well as legal and institutional limitations. However, the cohorts who will be near to retirement age ten to thirty years from now can have a variety of options not currently available. Those options will arise if different policies are adopted in the near and inter- mediate future. These policies can foster attitudinal changes, restructure institutional patterns, and bring about new provisions in our laws. As a result, the retirement decisions made by — and forced on — future cohorts can be less costly, and perhaps more satisfying, than those favored at this time. In other words, our contemporary working age cohorts have the possibility of creating options about the character of their life in the year 2000 or 2025. It remains to be seen if they can make these possibilities ripen into genuine choices.

General Factors Affecting Intercohort Exchanges

So far, we have been considering developments that directly bear on future intercohort exchanges. There are also other develop- ments that will have important, but more indirect effects. These developments, and some of their implications, deserve some discussion.

Much of the intercohort segregation that pervades modern Ameri- can life is related to the high value we attribute to privacy. Perhaps our strivings toward personal freedom stimulate us to exercise our freedom in ways that stifle others, and as a result (to protect our- selves) we place a high premium on privacy. But the pursuit of pri- vacy is economically costly. It requires larger houses, detached houses, dispersed residences, and a reliance on automobile transportation. All of these systems are highly energy-intensive. Yet America will be under increasing pressure to constrain its energy use. It is clear that future cohorts of Americans will need to learn how to live more intimately with one another.

One cause for the increase of our Gross National Product over the past twenty years — despite the lessening of the post-65 male labor force — has been the increase in the female labor force. Without such an increase, our already comparatively slow economic growth rate might have been further inhibited. If that had occurred, we would have had fewer goods to distribute to the elderly. But much of our more "simple" labor force expansion among females may already have occurred. In other words, further expansion in our female labor force could mean bringing in more "marginal" females — who may require expensive supplementary child-care help. This implies that maintaining growth in the future in order to support increasing proportions of old persons (not productively employed) may be more complicated than it was in the recent past.

The continuing increase in age segregation in America can generate a variety of complicating effects. It can develop ghettos of the aged, which could range from communities to whole states. Such patterns would make it harder to integrate the aged into the reciprocal life of the society. Simultaneously, by isolating working age and young cohorts from the aged, it can lessen understanding about the nature of aging, making workers less able to perceive and promote different policies that could improve their own old age. In other words, we can take only modest systemic steps to improve the old age of persons now at or near 65; and most of those steps will be largely economic measures. However, if we wish to reshape the social forces determining the general nature of old age, we must aim to shape the future of persons who are now (let us say) 45 or 50. But, when the aged are out of sight, then working cohorts (the majority of society) hear about them only as economic problems. As a result, the majority's perception of constructive new roles for the aged is diminished: when we are "out of touch" with a problem, our solutions are usually less appropriate.

There is, at the present time, discussion about encouraging older persons — often already retired — to return to school or college for additional formal education. Certainly, a retired person has the right to make such a choice. Still, we should critically analyze proposals to make such late-in-life learning a major activity of the aged. While there is a great deal of "new" knowledge which can be transmitted to the aged, and while there can be pleasure in reflecting on life in one's late maturity, many old persons possess wisdom which many younger teachers and students lack. Most societies recognize such wisdom as a social resource, and, instead of filling their elderly with factual information that they will have only a modest chance to use, they make teachers of them. Of course, enlisting the old in important teaching roles in our society would involve institutional adaptation and possibly represent a threat to some present teachers —

who may possess more information than wisdom. Still, it may be worth some reorganizing to increase our working store of wisdom.

Incidentally, when we talk of using large numbers of the aged as "teachers," we should recognize that lecturing in front of a class is only one way — and not necessarily the most imaginative way — of transmitting wisdom. Other teaching roles for the aged can include advising younger workers; talking and reminiscing with the young about courtship, marriage, child-rearing, finding a first job or a career; or otherwise assisting the inexperienced to learn — through thoughtful discussions — from someone who's been through life. I think the visions of large numbers of old as learners is also economically unrealistic. Hiring teachers is not cheap, and such costs are usually borne by working cohorts. And so, while recruiting large numbers of aged learners for education may serve the short-run institutional needs of a system searching for students, it will also significantly add to the increasing costs of maintaining retired persons. It is better to emphasize the responsibilities of the aged to pass on their wisdom, than to send them back to school like children — as if one learned nothing from life worth passing on to others. It is degrading and absurd.

A Forecast

A social and economic forecast derived from the preceding material in this chapter must contain some discouraging aspects. On one hand, the systems for socializing our children into adults committed to healthy reciprocity have declined in vitality. And the data about adolescent alienation recited in the Appendix offer support for this interpretation. These dysfunctional systems are driven by a variety of powerful forces, ranging from widespread public attitudes to patterns of school and suburban organization. On the other hand, these less adequately socialized cohorts will also be an important part of the American electorate that will be asked to enlarge support of the aged through remote, intangible, formally enforced reciprocity systems.

At the same time, older cohorts are increasingly being socialized to look at old age as a time for non-productive withdrawal. This withdrawal adds to the costs of their maintenance and makes their status less apparent.

Furthermore, it is obvious that systemic reverence for the past and the achievements of our ancestors is probably at an historic low in American society. Yet such reverence is the donation of the living to the Great Exchange. Without that donation, how can we hope for reverence after our own death? At the same time, America has as much need as ever — and perhaps more — for long-range commitments from citizens, both as voters and leaders. Lacking such general commitment, we may invest our national energies into short-sighted, fast gratification programs that generate anxiety rather than productive results. Meanwhile, action directed at our more serious public problems may be inordinately postponed.

To turn from the macro to the micro level, there is reason to foresee further decay of intercohort exchanges within families. Such decay can deprive family and personal life of much of its richness. Parenting can become so frustrating and sterile that couples who have committed themselves to parenthood may feel they have been "taken." Or adults may choose to avoid such "sterile" responsibilities. Then they may discover, late in their careers, that life outside a generational progression may be life without a future. We should not expect that innumerable private frustrations engendered by these patterns will simply be buried in each sufferer's psyche. It is just as likely that they will gradually seep out through diverse channels to corrode social life throughout society. Eventually, scapegoats will be discovered to absorb this anger and pain. Unfortunately, unlike the literal scapegoat — which was a domestic animal driven off into the wilderness to die — we have developed, in our times a tendency to transform other segments of our society into scapegoats. And so we may belittle and scorn one another to expiate personal sorrows. Perhaps, since these sorrows are partially the outcome of general social patterns, there may be some justice to such social criticism. However, the criticism is usually not directed at "real" causes, such as the frustrations of unreciprocated parenthood or non-parental marriage. And so we may end up injuring something beneficial, and preserving generally destructive policies.

Despite this comparatively bleak sketch, we cannot ignore important homeostatic elements in our society. As a democratic country, we have innumerable channels for the articulation of warnings and proposals about the challenges ahead. Equally importantly, almost all working age adults — the majority of our society — have a vital personal interest in the maintenance of healthy patterns of intercohort reciprocity. For they wish to lead long lives, and at the end of every such life lies the inevitable dependence of old age. The nature of that dependence will be largely determined by the character of their working years. During the twenty to forty years of their working and housekeeping life, they can decide the general policies that will govern the systems for the socialization of the young they are supporting as taxpayers and parents. Furthermore, working adults can help to determine — as voters, union members, co-workers, employers, stockholders, and family members — what norms will be in effect about retirement policies by the time they approach 65. As for the Great Exchange, our own expectations as to remembrance are now being decided by the socialization we are giving our young — both in society and in individual families.

Obviously, carrying out such constructive social change represents an ambitious task for our working age cohorts. But a rewarding old age — or the promise of remembrance after death — can never be purchased cheaply. And what we are buying is not only greater economic security, but even more precious goods: honor, respect, and dramatic evidence that our lives have made a difference to those we leave behind us.

Some Prescriptions

Let us now consider a series of summary prescriptions that might be applied by working age adults who wish to insure that their old age will be provided with true social security:

1. Rather than broadcasting the assumption that social security taxes should and will be steadily expanded to provide benefits to the aged, a contrary assumption should be propounded. That is, Congress should once again amend the Social Security Act to establish some future ceiling on the benefits provided in the Act. This prospective ceiling should be lower than the current benefits. The ceiling should go into effect at some predetermined future date (between ten to thirty years after the passage of the amendment). In effect, the ceiling would govern Congressional management of the social security tax rate during the intervening period. The appropriateness of proposed

changes in the tax rate before the date fixed for lowering would be affected by their relationship to that future lowered benefit rate.

The ceiling would aim to gradually lessen our society's (presently) growing reliance on social security and equivalent remote, formally enforced reciprocity systems as the chief support for the aged. Such systems would gradually be supplemented by more immediate, informally enforced systems. The creation of the ceiling would symbolize this shift, by dramatically emphasizing to future retirees that old age security does not come from the "blue," but from the conscious decisions and sacrifices of other human beings. Unlike the statement quoted earlier, which talked of social security benefits as an "obligation," the ceiling would warn the present that a politically revocable commitment is not an obligation in most colloquial senses. The passage of the ceiling would stimulate contemporary working age adults to reconsider their present taking-for-granted attitudes about social security. As a result, they might reflect about who will pay for their retirement, why will they do it, and what can be done now to insure they will make such choices in the future? Conversely, the present implicit popular assumptions about social security — that we will just expand it when we need more — discourages serious intercohort socialization to reciprocity. Indeed, the assumptions raise the danger of future dramatic — and irresolvable — intercohort conflicts. And, if such conflicts do occur, they will actually be the "fault" of the cohorts of the (future) aged, who failed to make the emotional sacrifices necessary to socialize their young properly.

2. Formal education systems must be restructured to increase greatly the number and variety of tangible, immediate, continuous, informally enforced exchanges that occur in their operations. Some of these exchanges can be among students, either intracohort or intercohort, e.g., tutoring, using crossing guards, presenting dramatic performances to entertain others, helping to maintain the school. Some of them can be between students and teachers, or among teachers, e.g., the use of aides and lunchroom helpers. They can take the form of increased tangible teacher/teacher cooperation. Or they can be between the school and the external community, e.g., students maintaining public gardens, fundraising for community projects, and helping the

aged, or parents and other adults volunteering to help in the school.

3. Older persons should be assisted and encouraged (and, if necessary, pressured) to continue working after 65. Attaining this end will require the restructure of some jobs, and, where appropriate, the pay rates. The development of this policy will have a number of beneficial outcomes: it will lower the cost of care of the aged; it will diminish the forces supporting age segregation; it will offer the young a model of continuous reciprocity, rather than the present aspirations of an old age free from responsibility (perhaps an infantile aspiration); and it will increase the political and social power of the aged, since power essentially flows from engagement and contact, not from withdrawal.

4. We should pursue policies to discourage residential and geographic age segregation. In many modern environments, the withdrawal of the aged to segregated communities is partially the outcome of their seeking a more proximate communal life than is available in many "non-neighborhoods." While housing arrangements can be redesigned to discourage such segregation, and to reinforce richer community life, other systems for promoting community also need to be devised. Perhaps various types of shared and jointly operated services can serve to foster community: older neighbors undertaking child-care responsibilities; community gardens maintained by residents; property management and maintenance handled by community members. Of course, planning and maintaining such services will take some give on the part of all, but that is what reciprocity is about. On a macrocosmic level, state and federal tax and fund-granting policies can be devised that discourage the development of homogeneous environments. These policies would rest on the rationale that such segregation creates forms of social imbalance that ultimately produce deleterious effects within the commonwealth. Incidentally, we have not thus far mentioned legislation prohibiting age discrimination by employers. Such an approach involves difficult problems. There are often differences in capability between elderly and younger workers. And so the proposition that no age discrimination is justified becomes problematic, if it is premised on the lack of age differences. It may be generally wiser — and more justified — to say that both employers and the aged should jointly engage in adaptation to increase employment of the elderly.

5. We need to create more systems for generally increasing immediate, continuous, informally enforced intercohort exchanges. In business, older employees should be designated as mentors of younger employees (which is not the same as being their supervisors). Peter Drucker has described and highly praised the operation of this process in Japanese industry.[9] In school, teachers should have continuing significant responsibility for, and authority over — during each student's entire period of enrollment in a school — a small number of students, for whom they act as advisors. All possible steps should be taken to increase the vitality of youth-serving organizations relying on adult volunteers, i.e., informally enforced donations. Schools can strive to have students become more familiar with non-family adults in their communities, e.g., writing term papers based on interviewing retired persons, war veterans, or couples who are celebrating their silver wedding anniversary.[10] Businesses, unions, churches, and service groups might "adopt" schools, to provide them not with money, but with visits and exchange visits; and students could be stimulated to "repay" the courtesies they receive.

6. As for the Great Exchange, we will stimulate the young to sacrifice for the future and to honor the aged to the extent we participate with them in revering the past. When Washington's birthday is a three-day weekend, Columbus Day an occasion for special sales, and Martin Luther King's birthday is used to get the students out of school so there can be a teacher training session, we deliver profound instructions to our young. If we want them to learn otherwise, we must teach by our conduct, or we will suffer from their ignorance.

In Japan they have recently created a national holiday in honor of the aged.[11] But there is no sense in our creating such a holiday (the word is derived from "holy day") for another three-day weekend, or to let students out of school and leave them with time to kill. Serious holidays require adult planning, so that emotionally significant things happen on such occasions. In some ways, a holiday, if well managed, will be more "work" for many persons — paraders, performers, orators — than a workday. But workdays only produce workday goods and servies: holidays can produce motivation and community.

7. There is an obvious relationship between our macrocosmic systems for mediating intercohort reciprocity and the general growth of our public systems for mediating donations to dependent citizens.

And that growth has been demonstrated by the steady enlargement of the proportion of our Gross National Product distributed by governmental agencies. These remote, widespread, governmental reciprocity systems rest on many of the same values and premises that underlie our current systems of intercohort exchanges: the promotion of privacy; the concealment of dependency; and the naive ignorance of a powerful tendency toward human selfishness.

It is unlikely that we can strengthen immediate, informally enforced systems of intercohort exchange without simultaneously becoming engaged with revising (and presumably lessening) the general role of government as a system for mediating other forms of donations to dependent persons and groups. The prospect of such a shrinkage of the government's role in these donations may be greeted with dis-ease and fear among groups who receive the donations. And it will surely provoke angry responses from certain professionals whose families are supported through their employment by such mediating agencies. Still, we are talking about gradual change, and only about transforming intangible dependency — the current situation — into tangible dependency.

There is an anomaly surrounding this matter that warrants discussion. Many professionals and intellectuals seem quite prepared to argue that dependent donees of such programs in general, have a high sense of public responsibility, i.e., they take only the benefits they have "earned" and do all they can to support themselves. However, these same defenders of donees fear that independent donors, if their "obligations" to assist the needy are only informally enforced, will not make appropriate payments. The proposition seems to be that only people in need have decency; all others must be coerced, covertly taxed and otherwise harrassed into displaying charity and love. Perhaps a more generous — or realistic — vision of human nature might accept the need for immediate monitoring of dependent donees, and more faith in the willingness of independent donors to give. If we accept this vision, we will be more prone to move to reliance on proximate informal systems.

The prescriptions just outlined have been portrayed with great generality. It would be unrealistic to sketch such long-range, ambitious proposals in greater detail. Furthermore, we do not know a great deal about how to carry out some of these proposals at this time,

e.g., the restructuring of jobs for the elderly, or the encouragement of vital intercohort communities. This understandable ignorance
argues for attention to one important procedural factor. We must
greatly increase the power of local communities, governmental units,
and individual states to engage in adaptation and planning to improve
intercohort reciprocity, and socialization to reciprocity.

At this time, the most severe handicap to such flexibility is not a
lack of resources, but the constraints on local and regional action
imposed by the existence of national and extra-local systems. The
fact is that many of the important activities in our communities are
closely tied to integrated national networks. Thus, social security
is a national program. Many employers are nationwide corporations.
While school policies are allegedly locally decided, most of these
policies are the outcome of a national consensus and various federally
(and state) enforced mandates and prohibitions. The policies applied
in many welfare programs are determined by federal legislation. The
federal courts routinely intervene in local areas of decisionmaking
to promote egalitarian aims, i.e., to insure that certain uniform
national policies are applied. Our national media networks provoke
the development of widespread common attitudes about issues such
as reciprocity.

The sum effect of these various forces is to greatly diminish
social adaptability. Many localized "experiments" must be analyzed
and "adjudicated" by conflicting interest groups throughout the
entire nation before they can get off the ground.[12] Only if we can
somehow inhibit and control our desire to manage and solve all things
nationally, will we be able to develop productive adaptations to the
challenge of intercohort reciprocity.

APPENDIX

The following information consists of the most recent available aggregated, long-term, national statistics about certain trends in youth conduct. The presentation is brief, since I have written extensively about these developments elsewhere.[1] The statistics are about whites who, as our majority class, are seen as experiencing an advantaged status.

*** Between 1950 and 1976, the rate of death by suicide by white males, age 15 through 19, increased 260%. The suicide rate for older adults remained relatively stable during this period.

*** Between 1959 and 1976, the rate of death by homicide for white males, ages 15 through 19, increased 177%. Most of the assailants were other white male adolescents. This was the highest rate of increase for any group of white males.

*** Between 1950 and 1976, the estimated number of illegitimate births for unmarried white females, ages 15 through 19, increased 143%. The rate of increase among these young persons far exceeded any increases among older females.

*** The level of white adolescent illegitimacy is at the highest rate in this century; the levels of homicide and suicide are about 10% below the century's maximums, attained in 1975.

*** In an affluent suburban community, the number of seventh grade boys who began drinking during the previous year increased from 52% in 1969 to 72% in 1973. A 1974 national survey disclosed that 24% of the respondents of both sexes between 13 and 19 reported being drunk four or more times during the previous year.

*** Between 1957 and 1974, the number of delinquency cases disposed of by U.S. juvenile courts increased 96%.

*** In two surveys of national samples of students in American research universities, the proportion of students who admitted engaging in some form of cheating rose from 5.4% in 1969 to 9.8% in 1976 — an 87% increase.

*** Between 1960 and 1973, throughout the country, arrests of males under 18 for narcotics violations increased 1,288%.

***   National surveys report no significant declines in levels of youth drug use, and surveys of high school graduating classes of 1975 and 1977 found that the percentage of males who had used marijuana before tenth grade had increased from 18.2% to 30.6%.

***   A variety of surveys of youth attitudes and conduct between 1948 and 1973 have disclosed a steady increase in attitudes evincing withdrawal, cynicism, loneliness, and hostility to authority. Two national surveys of adult attitudes found that the level of tension and worry among young adults (ages 21 through 39) increased from about 30% (in 1957) to 50% (in 1976). These developing attitudes are clearly inconsistent with both a serious acceptance of social responsibility and a sense of wholesome self-respect.

***   Two careful surveys of school crime and violence both concluded that the level of school crime has increased gradually since (about) 1955, and that, if the increase has leveled off, there has been no sign of any decrease. Students are in more risk of being criminally victimized in school than in any other environment where they ordinarily spend their time.

The patterns of increases revealed in these statistics also generally apply to blacks. However, there are minor differences, which may be more related to the lower socio-economic status of blacks (as generally compared to white) than to the issue of race *per se*. Essentially, while all the black statistics go up like those of the whites, the homicide and illegitimacy rates for black adolescents are higher than whites, and their suicide rate is lower.

These distressing statistics justify the conclusion that there have been substantial changes in the feelings and conduct of American youth over the past twenty to twenty-five years. And, obviously, these changes extend far beyond the conduct explicitly described by the data. For instance, the suicide rate is only a direct measure of "successful" suicides that have been detected; however, it also indirectly measures undetected suicides, attempted suicides, and severe depressions. When measured suicide rates go up, we should assume that all the other indices similarly shift.

The data do not mean that all — or most — American youths are distraught. We are a large country, and there are many pockets of health maintained by individual families and/or wholesome local institutions. Still, there has been an indisputably significant deterioration.

The conduct and attitudes described by the statistics can be characterized in terms easily understood by laymen. The statistics demonstrate the steady spread of loneliness, boredom, purposelessness, selfishness, and anger among our young. These shifts are understandably accompanied by a decline in the capability of the young to accept delayed gratification, I describe the attitude changes in these harsh terms because the understanding is that persons prone to hurt themselves or others grievously, or to explore drugs or sex irresponsibly, are likely to be leading emotionally empty lives. They have very little to do that is worthwhile, what they have to do that is constructive is not important, and they do not know how to do it well.

These remarks should not be construed as criticism of our children and youths. It is true that the conduct and attitudes just sketched are undesirable. But young people, in general, do what they are "told" to do by adults and adult institutions. If adult institutions treat them in a trivial and disengaged fashion, they respond appropriately. Of course, young people will not say "We don't want to be treated trivially!" Indeed, they may even explicitly say, "Adults aren't leaving us alone enough," or "We aren't permitted to do what we want." But adults who try to socialize the young should interpret what they say, rather than simply respond literally. The young, when "left alone," are increasingly prone to engage in activities harmful to themselves and others. One should interpret this conduct to "say" they really want engagement and consequential demands. Satisfying such a request means hard — but gratifying — work for many adults.

REFERENCES

Introduction

1. Jeremy Bentham, quoted in A. V. Dicey, *Law and Public Opinion in England* (New York: Macmillan Company, 1905), p. 171.

Chapter 1
On Reciprocity

1. Alvin W. Gouldner, "The Norm of Reciprocity," *American Sociological Review* 25, no. 2 (April, 1960) p. 176.

2. There is an extensive literature on the subject of reciprocity. Some pertinent works include: Peter M. Blau, *Exchange and Power in Social Life* (New York: John Wiley, 1967); Takeno Doi, *The Anatomy of Dependence* (New York: Kodansha International, 1973), translated by John Bestor; Gouldner, "The Norm of Reciprocity": 161-177; Peter Kropotkin, *Mutual Aid* (New York: New York University Press, 1972); Marcel Mauss, *The Gift* (New York: The Free Press, 1954), translated by Ian Cunningham; Karl Polanyi, *Primitive Archaic and Modern Economies,* ed. George Dalton (Garden City, New York: Doubleday Anchor, 1968); and Lucius Annaeus Seneca, "On Benefits," vol. 3, *Seneca's Moral Essays* (Cambridge: Harvard University Press, 1936), translated by John W. Basore. See also various entries under "cooperation," "exchange," and "reciprocity" in *International Encyclopedia of the Social Sciences* (New York: Macmillan, 1968).

3. The shift toward formally structured exchanges was first remarked by Henry Sumner Maine, *Ancient Law* (New York: Henry Holt and Co., 1906), originally published in 1861, pp. 303 et. seq.

4. See, e.g., Institute of Economic Affairs, *The Economics of Charity* (London: The Institute of Economic Affairs, 1973) and Michael Young and Peter Willmott, *Family and Kinship in East* (London, Baltimore: Penguin Books, 1965).

5. For an extensive compilation of materials on the natural "goodness" or "selfishness" of man, see Donald T. Campbell, "On the Conflicts Between Biological and Social Evolution and Between Psychology and

Moral Tradition," *American Psychologist* 30 (1975): 1103-1126, and the succeeding symposium on that article, "The War Between the Words: Biological Versus Social Evolution and Some Related Issues," Lauren G. Wispe and James N. Thompson, eds. *American Psychologist* 31 (1976): 341-384.

6. Jean Piaget has proposed that infants "naturally" develop toward progressively higher levels of reciprocity and morality. Still, he also concedes that "even the most rational of adults does not subject to his 'moral experience' more than an infinitesimal proportion of the rules that hedge around him." *The Moral Judgement of the Child* (New York: The Free Press, 1965), translated by Marjorie Gabain, p. 96. If we accept Piaget's concession, then presumably most of a child's learning about reciprocity consists not of "naturally" developing, but of absorbing social conventions. And, if they are not absorbed, his personal "moral experience" will leave him unequipped for social life.

7. Many readers will realize that this discussion merely restates the numerous philosophical arguments that first came to prominence in the writings of Rosseau (see, e.g., *Discourse on the Origins of Inequality*), and that have been continuing ever since. For one contemporary formulation of these issues, see Robert A. Nisbet, *The Social Bond* (New York: Alfred Knopf, 1970).

8. For an example applying reciprocal concepts to complex bargaining situtations, see Thomas C. Schelling, *The Strategy of Conflict* (Cambridge: Harvard University Press, 1960).

9. To read a typical ethnography in which this process is described, see Margaret Read, *Children of Their Fathers* (New York: Holt, Rinehart and Winston, 1968). Tribal members spent a great deal of their time in informal interfamily discussions about principles of child-rearing; in effect, there was (a) a tribal norm about these principles, (b) a similar intrafamily norm, consciously worked out and followed by many families, and (c) an occasional "deviant" family, which was under social pressures to conform to tribal norms.

10. A great deal of work in the analysis of basic structures of social reciprocity has been done by George C. Homans, *The Human*

Group (New York: Harcourt, Brace and Co., 1950) and *Social Behavior: Its Elementary Forms* (New York: Harcourt, Brace, Jovanovich, 1974), revised edition.

11. Of course, some writers have described environments where the "whole" community participates in the rearing of comparatively young children (see, e.g., Phillipe Aries, *Centuries of Childhood* (New York: Alfred Knopf, 1962). However, these "communities" were essentially small, parochial, stable environments, where common understandings could grow, and were protected. It is true that some of these community involvement principles are followed throughout large, contemporary societies (e.g., in the Soviet Union), but perhaps it is no coincidence that such societies are typically totalitarian, where the circulation of dissonant information is tightly constrained.

12. For some amplification of these themes, see Edward A. Wynne, "Accountable to Whom" *Society* 13, no. 2 (January/February 1976): 30-37.

13. A useful general mode of this process of approaching adulthood and leavetaking is contained in S. N. Eisenstadt, *From Generation to Generation* (New York: The Free Press, 1956).

14. For a general discussion of the role of symbols, ceremonies, and role models in socialization, see, e.g., Orrin L. Klapp, *The Collective Search for Identity* (New York: Holt, Rinehart and Winston, 1969).

15. *Deuteronomy,* 25:9; see also *The Book of Ruth.*

16. The proposal that age groups (as compared to generations) be used as the basic unit of analysis was first made by Karl Mannheim, "The Problem of Generations," in *Essays on the Sociology of Knowledge,* ed. Paul Kecskemieti (London: Routledge and Kegan, Paul, 1952), pp. 276-320.

17. For much useful discussion about patterns of cohort distribution, see Matilda White Riley, Marily Johnson and Anne Foner, vol. 3 of *Aging and Society, A Sociology of Age Stratification* (New York: Russell Sage, 1972).

18. For discussions of diverse structures affecting the status of the aged, see, e.g., Donald O. Cowgill and Lowell D. Holmes, eds., *Aging and Modernization* (New York: Appleton-Century, 1972) and

Leo W. Simmons, *The Role of the Aged in Primitive Society* (New Haven, Connecticut: Yale University Press, 1945).

Chapter 2
Reciprocity in Pre-Industrial Societies

1. M. H. Abrams, *et. al.,* eds., *The Norton Anthology of English Literature* (Revised), vol. 1 (New York: W. W. Norton, 1968), p. 81.

2. For an interesting work cataloging acts of animal reciprocity, see Kropotkin, *Mutual Aid.*

3. For one work discussing the implications of genetically determined patterns, see Edward O. Wilson, *On Human Nature* (Cambridge, Mass.: Harvard University Press, 1978).

4. Edward O. Wilson, "Competitive and Aggressive Behavior," in *Man and Beast: Comparative Social Behavior,* ed. J. S. Eisenberg and Wilton S. Dillon (Washington, D.C.: Smithsonian Institution Press, 1971), p. 207.

5. For early basic writings on these themes, see Maine, *Ancient Law* and Ferdinand Tonnies, *Community and Society* (East Lansing, Mich.: Michigan State University Press, 1964), translated by Charles P. Loomis. For a recent authoritative survey, see George Dalton, *Economic Anthropology and Development* (New York: Basic Books, 1971) and Dalton, "Economic Anthropology," *American Behavioral Scientist* 13, no. 5 (May/June, 1977): 635-656.

6. Karl Polyani, *The Great Transformation* (New York: Farr and Rinehard, 1944). For a useful summation of Polyani's diverse writings on this topic, see Polyani, *Primitive Economies.*

7. Polyani, *Primitive Economies,* p. 71.

8. Raymond Firth, *Economics of the New Zealand Maori* (Wellington, New Zealand: A. R. Shearer, 1972), p. 309.

9. A. Rosman and P. Rubel, *Feasting with Mine Enemy* (New York: Columbia University Press, 1971).

10. For an extended statement of what I term a "naively" voluntaristic position, see Richard M. Titmuss, *The Gift Relationship* (New York: Pantheon, 1971). Interestingly, Titmuss' provocative work

has been criticized from two directions: (a) that it is wrong to call "gifts" purely voluntary when they are given in the expectation of some reciprocal counterdonation, and (b) that the gift situation described by Titmuss — in which blood donors contribute without receiving cash payments — was medically more inefficient than a payment-for-blood situation. The first criticism is argued in Institute of Economic Affairs, *The Economics of Charity* (London: Institute, 1973). The second is presented in Harvey M. Sapolsky and Stan N. Finkelstein, "Blood Policy Revisted, *The Public Interest* 46 (Winter, 1977): 15-28.

11. The many writings of Erving Goffman provide a sensitive survey of the human need for contact, observation, and control over those who are routinely proximate to us. See, e.g., Goffman, *The Presentation of Self in Everyday Life* (Garden City, New York: Doubleday/Anchor, 1959).

12. For a typical example of such an act of recognition, see the description of the Aztec emperor Montezuma by Bernal Diaz del Castillo in *True History of the Conquest of Mexico* (Ann Arbor, Mich.: University Microfilms, 1966).

13. Maine, *Ancient Law*, p. 303, *et seq.*

14. Aristotle, *The Ethics* (London: George, Allen and Unwin, 1953), translated by J. A. K. Thompson; Marcus Tullius Cicero, *On Duties* (Indianapolis: Bobbs-Merrill, 1974) translated by Harry G. Edinger; and Seneca, *On Benefits.*

15. Seneca, *On Benefits,* p. 241.

16. For significant discussion of the phenomena, see Bronislaw Malinowski, *The Argonauts of the Western Pacific* (New York: E. P. Dutton, 1961), and Mauss, *The Gift.* For a more recent work on the same theme, see Erik Schwimmer, *Exchange in the Social Structure of the Orokaiva* (London: Hurst, 1973).

17. For a review of the role of the donations in classic Greece and Rome, see, Arthur R. Hands, *Charities and Social Aid in Greece and Rome* (Ithica, New York: Cornell University Press, 1968). Ironically, the title of this authoritative work reflects a potential misnomer, since the "modern" connotation of charity — an apparently

unreciprocated act — would have seemed perverse to the classic Greeks and Romans.

18. Brian Tierney, *Medieval Poor Law* (Berkeley: University of California Press, 1959).

19. Matthew, 25: 34-45.

20. For one analysis of this powerful tendency toward selfishness, see Ellen C. Dunn, *The Concept of Ingratitude in Renaissance English Moral Philosophy* (Ann Arbor, Mich,: University Microfilms, 1968).

21. George Unwin, *The Guilds and Companies of London* (New York: Barnes and Noble, 1964).

22. Eisenstadt, *From Generation to Generation.*

23. For an example of an ethnographic study describing age grading in operation in a specific tribe, see Monica Wilson, *Good Company* (Boston: Beacon Press, 1963). While the "youth groups" in the tribe practiced a large degree of self-government, the general outlines of that government were set by adults. For example, "serious" disputes between members of the "boys' village" were settled by the headsman of the adult community, p. 184.

24. Benjamin White, "The Economic Importance of Children in a Japanese Village," in *Population and Social Organization,* ed. Moni Nag (Chicago: Aldine, 1975), pp. 127-146. For other example of the genuine efficiency of many child workers, see William N. Stephens, *Our Children Should be Working* (Springfield, Ill.: Charles C. Thomas, 1979).

25. See, e.g., Cowgill and Holmes, *Aging* and Simmons, *Role of the Aged.*

26. Interestingly enough, research on scientific creativity in modern society discloses that scientists working the the "harder sciences (e.g., physics, mathematics) tend to make their significant discoveries during their early lives, while scientists in the more socially oriented fields (e.g., sociology, history) ripen much later in life. See, e.g., K. Warner Schaie, "Age Changes in Adult Intelligence," in *Aging,* Diana Woodruff and James E. Birren (New York: D. Van Nostrand, 1975), pp. 111-124. Presumably, social scientists must live through certain life experiences, as well as read books, before they have the knowledge needed for important creative work.

27. Matilda White Riley, John W. Riley, Jr., and Marilyn Johnson, *An Inventory of Research Findings,* vol. 1, *Aging and Society* (New York: Russell Sage, 1968), p. 25.

28. Gy. Acsadi and J. Neneskeri, *History of Human Life Span and Mortality* (Budapest, Hungary: Akademiai Kiado, 1970), p. 251.

29. Peter Laslett, *The World We Have Lost* (London: Methuen and Company, 1965).

30. Richard A. Easterlin, "Does Money Buy Happiness?" *The Public Interest* 30 (Winter 1973): 3-10.

Chapter 3
The Great Exchange

1. Fustel De Coulanges, *The Ancient City* (Boston: Lathrop, Les and Shepard, 1873), p. 61.

2. For other works presenting this perspective, see Emily M. Ahern, *The Cult of the Dead in a Chinese Village* (Stanford, Ca.: Stanford University Press, 1973); de Coulanges, *The Ancient City;* William A. Douglass, *Death in Murilaga* (Seattle, Wash.: University of Washington Press, 1969); Johnb Morley, *Death, Heaven, and the Victorians* (Pittsburgh: University of Pittsburgh Press, 1971); and W. Lloyd Warner, *The Living and the Dead* (New Haven: Yale University Press, 1959).

3. T. S. Eliot, "Murder in the Cathedral," in *The Complete Poems and Plays, 1909-1950* (New York: Harcourt, Brace and World, 1958), pp. 191-192.

4. An interesting presentation of these themes is found in Auguste Comte, *A General View of Positivism* (Dubuque, Iowa: Brown Reprints, 1971), first published in 1848. Comte observed that "To live in others is, in the truest sense of the word, life" (p. 368). And so he proposed the development of social systems in which our lives would be structured so as to encourage others yet-to-be-born to live in — and through — us.

5. A useful outline and analysis of these identity shaping devices is contained in Orwin L. Klapp, *The Collective Search for Identity* (New York: Holt, Rinehart and Winston, 1969).

6. After the development of literacy, may traditional societies, and institutions in such societies, established the office of chronicler: that officer's task was to record chronologically the important events in the day-to-day life of the system, and to relate those events to the persons involved. Thomas a Kempis, a medieval monk and writer of devotional literature, was the chronicler of his monastary. On his death, the succeeding chronicler made the following entry in the chronicle about his prececessor: "In the same year, on the Feast of St. James the Less, after Compline, our Brother Thomas Haemerken, born at Kempen, a town in the diocese of Cologne, departed from this earth. He was in the 92nd year of his age, and 63rd of his religious clothing, and the 58th of his priesthood. In his youth, he was a disciple, at Deventer, of Master Florentius, who sent him to his own brother, who was then Prior of Mount S. Agnes. Thomas, who was then 20 years of age, received the habit from his brother at the close of six years probation, and from the outset of his monastic life he endured great poverty, temptations, and labours. He copied out our Bible and various other books, some of which were used by the convent, and others were sold. Further, for the instruction of the young, he wrote various little treatises in a plain and simple style, which in reality were great and important works, both in doctrine and efficacy for good. He had an especial devotion to the Passion of Our Lord, and understood admirably how to comfort those afflicted by interior trials and temptations. Finally, having reached a ripe old age, he was afflicted with dropsy of the limbs, slept in the Lord in the year of 1471, and was buried in the east side of the cloister, by the side of Peter Herbert." Thomas a Kempis, *The Imitation of Christ* (Baltimore: Penguin Classics, 1952), pp. 22-23.

7. Read, *Children of Their Fathers,* p. 124.

8. Traditional Chinese society, for example, dedicated a high level of resources to reverencing the past. See Ahern, *The Cult of the Dead.*

9. *The Complete Writings of Thucydides* (New York: The Modern Library, 1951), p. 103 ff.

10. Presumably, one purpose of the English laws of primogeniture and entail was to maintain the persistent identity of families and

family estates — and to provide reinforcement for long-range aspirations among prominent citizens, who could readily aspire to remembrance after death as a result of the social patterns maintained by such laws.

11. A sensitive portrayal of the implicit burdens generated by intergenerational reciprocity is contained in *I Never Promised You a Rose Garden*. The book is a novel, which describes the emotions felt by a mentally disturbed adolescent toward the considerations shows her by her parents and other relatives. "Among equals gratitude is reciprocal; her gratitude to these Titans, who called themselves average and were unaware of their own tremendous strength in being able to live, only made her feel more lost, inept, and lonely than ever." Joanne Greenberg (New York: Signet Books, 1964), p. 211.

12. See, e.g., Diane Ravitch, *The Revisionists Revised* (New York: Basic Books, 1978).

Chapter 4
Exchanges in Industrial Society

1. "President Pierce's Veto of Miss Dix's Bill," in *Public Welfare Administration in the United States,* ed. Sophonisba P. Breckenridge (Chicago: University of Chicago Press, 1938), p. 221.

2. For various descriptions of these developments, see Maurice Bruce, *The Coming of the Welfare State* (London: B. T. Batsford, 1967); Karl de Schweinitz, *England's Road to Social Security* (Philadelphia: University of Pennsylvania Press, 1943); W. K. Jordan, *Philanthropy in England, 1480-1600* (New York: Russell Sage, 1959); Samuel Mencher, *Poor Law to Poverty Program* (Pittsburgh: University of Pittsburgh Press, 1967); Ivy Pinchbeck and Margaret Hewith, eds., *Children in English Society,* vol. 1, *From Tudor Times to the Eighteenth Century* (Toronto: University of Toronto Press, 1969); and Walter I. Trattner, *From Poor Law to Welfare State* (New York: The Free Press, 1974).

3. Recall the nursery rhyme, "Hark! Hark! The dogs do bark! The beggars are coming to town!" Presumably, the visitation of a small

rural community by a group of "sturdy vagabonds" was not seen in a reassuring light.

4. Great Britain, *Poor Law Commissioners' Report of 1834* (London: His Majesty's Stationery Office, 1905), pp. 11, ff. See also Bruce, *The Coming of the Welfare State;* de Schweinitz, *England's Road to Social Security;* and Mencher, *Poor Law to Welfare State.*

5. Jordan, *Philanthropy,* p. 140.

6. Jordan, *Philanthropy,* p. 169.

7. Jordan, *Philanthropy,* p. 221.

8. Jordan, *Philanthropy,* p. 291.

9. Bernard Bailyn, *Education and the Forming of American Society* (Chapel Hill: University of North Carolina Press, 1960).

10. David J. Rothman and Sheila M. Rothman, eds., *Sources of American Social Tradition* (New York: Basic Books, 1975), p. 24.

11. See, Bailyn, *Education and the Forming of American Society* and Lawrence A. Cremin, *American Education: The Colonial Experience* (New York: Harper and Row, 1970), pp. 170 ff.

12. Rothman, *Sources of American Social Tradition,* pp. 52-53.

13. Rothman, *Sources of American Social Tradition,* p. 146.

14. Rothman, *Sources of American Social Tradition,* p. 142.

15. See, e.g., Colin Geer, *The Great School Legend* (New York: Basic Books, 1972).

16. Diane Ravitch, *The Great School Wars* (New York: Basic Books, 1974), p. 17.

17. For sources, see, *Great Britain, Report of 1834;* Bruce, *The Coming of the Welfare State;* de Schweinitz, *England's Road to Social Security;* and Mencher, *Poor Law to Welfare State.*

18. Eric J. Hobsbawm, in *Standards of Living in England During the Industrial Revolution,* ed. A. J. Taylor (London: Melkner, 1977), p. 69.

19. While several writers have described and commented on the work of Chalmers, the best treatment is N. Masterson, ed., *Chalmers*

on Charity (Westminster, England: Archibald and Constable and Co., 1900). This book is essentially an edited version of Chalmers' numerous writings.

20. Masterman, *Chalmers,* p. 312.

21. For signs of Chalmers' later influence, see, e.g., Josephine Shaw Lowell, *Public Relief and Private Charity* (New York: G. P. Putnam, 1884), and Charles Stewart Loch, *Charity and Social Life* (London: Macmillan and Co., 1910).

22. Masterman, *Chalmers,* p. 332.

23. Masterman, *Chalmers,* p. 333.

24. Maine, *Ancient Law.*

25. On the obligation of religiously motivated donors to give so as to produce good effects on donees — and not merely to practice charity — see Tierney, *Medieval Poor Law.*

26. Duke de la Rochefoucauld, *Maxims* (London: Oxford University Press, 1940), translated by F. G. Stevens.

27. See Chapter 3, note 11.

28. This analysis is merely a restatement of the basic principles of behavioral psychology: we learn to repeat conduct that is positively reinforced, and when we receive "benefits," we attempt to "learn" and repeat the conduct that will maintain the flow of benefits.

29. Neil J. Smelser, *Social Change in the Industrial Revolution* (Chicago: University of Chicago Press, 1959).

30. P.H.J.P. Gosden, *The Friendly Societies in England* (Manchester, England: Manchester University Press, 1961). Similar societies operated in America during approximately the same period.

31. Great Britain, *Report of 1834.*

32. Mark Balug, "The Myth of the Old Poor Law, and the Making of the New," *Journal of Economic History,* 23 (June 1963): 131-184 and Balug, "The Poor Law Reexamined," *Journal of Economic History,* 24 (June 1964): 229-245.

33. See, e.g., Bruce, *The Coming of the Welfare State,* and de Schweinitz, *England's Road to Social Security,* pp. 88 ff., which also cites the concurring opinions of various social interventionists.

34. David Owen, *English Philanthropy, 1660-1960* (Cambridge: Harvard/Belknap Press, 1964), pp. 146 ff.

35. See Superintendent of Public Schools, City of Chicago, *Annual Reports, 1854-1890* (Chicago Board of Education, 1854-1890). Of course, at the present time, such business contributions are sometimes made at the college and graduate school level. But this shift in practices essentially represents a withdrawal of non-professional adults from proximate exchanges with children and adolescents (i.e., elementary and high school students) in preference to relationships with college professors, administrators and older students.

36. Robert N. Bremner, *American Philanthropy* (Chicago: University of Chicago Press, 1960), p. 111.

37. Andrew Carnegie, *Autobiography* (New York: Houghton, Mifflin, 1920).

38. Bremner, *American Philanthropy,* pp. 80 ff.

39. J. N. Larned, *The Life and Work of William Pryor Letchworth* (New York: Houghton, Mifflin, 1912), p. 114.

40. Owen, *English Philanthropy,* pp. 479 ff.

41. Owen, *English Philanthropy,* p. 481.

42. For examples of such activities, see Robert H. Bremner, ed., *Children and Youth in America,* vol. 2 (Cambridge: Harvard University Press, 1971); Bremner, *Philanthropy;* and Roy Lubove, *The Professional Altruist* (Cambridge: Harvard University Press, 1965). For a revisionist perspective on such activities, see Anthony M. Platt, *The Child Savers* (Chicago: University of Chicago Press, 1969).

43. An interesting example of this aspiration for after-death remembrance is found in the burial instructions left by William Pryor Letchworth. In a letter to his brother he said, "I would like my remains to be placed in a rough-hewn stone sarcophagus, after the general design of that illustrated in the sixth edition of the *Life of Mary Jemison,* page 274. The sarcophagus I desire to have taken from the Blue Stone Quarry, on the Genesee River, a few miles above Portageville. I desire that on the ground above it there should be laid a perfectly plan slab, after the style of that shown in the enclosed

illustration taken from the April number of *Country Life in America,* page 731, upon which slab shall be inscribed my name and the date of my birth and decease, only. If practicable, I desire that the slab be taken from the hard rock of the upper strata of Table Rock at the Lower Falls [on his estate near the Genessee River] which if I remember rightly, is from twelve to sixteen inches thick. I think this slab had best be placed directly upon the surface of the ground, without masonry underneath it, the inclination to be the same as the ground surrounding it." Larned, *Letchworth,* p. 421. Incidentally, during Letchworth's life, among his many activities, he helped to organize a residential school for delinquent and abandoned boys: it was named "Letchworth Village" in his honor.

44. See, e.g., Robert J. Havighurst, *Growing Up in River City* (New York: John Wiley, 1962), pp. 131 ff. and August de Belmont Hollingshead, *Elmstown's Youth* (New York: John Wiley, 1949), p. 272.

45. For discussion of these developments by contemporary and modern writers see, e.g., de Schweinitz, *England's Road to Social Security;* Loch, *Social Life;* Lowell, *Charity;* Lubove, *The Professional Altruist;* Mencher, *Poor Law to Poverty Program;* Owen, *English Philanthropy;* Platt, *The Child Savers;* and Emily Townsend, *The Case Against the Charity Organization Society* (London: The Fabian Soceity, 1911).

46. See e.g., Richard Hofstadter, *Social Darwinism and American Thought* (Boston: The Beacon Press, 1959).

47. For discussion about the individualistic tradition of American unions during much of the life of the American Federation of Labor, see Hace Sorel Tischler, *From Self-Reliance to Social Security* (Port Washington, New York: Kennikat Press, 1971).

48. The term "demographic revolution" was used by Acsadi and Neneskeri, *Life Span,* pp. 259 et seq. The quoted data are derived from Acsadi and Neneskeri; Louis I. Dublin and Alfred J. Latka, *Length of Life* (New York: Ronald Press, 1936), p. 65; and Riley *et al., Research Findings,* pp. 21, 424.

49. John G. Turnbull, *The Changing Faces of Economic Insecurity* (Minneapolis: University of Minnesota Press, 1966), p. 48.

50. For discussion of these themes, see Loch, *Charity;* Lubove, *The Professional Altruist;* and Mencher, *Poor Law to Poverty Program.*

51. Edward T. Devine, "Pensions for Mothers" in Bremner, *Children,* p. 379. Devine was secretary of the Charity Organization Society of New York City.

52. Commission on the Relief of Widowed Mothers, *Report* (Albany, New York: Commission, 1914), pp. 152-155.

53. U.S. Children's Bureau, *Mother's Aid, 1931* (Washington: Government Printing Office, 1934), pp. 6-24.

54. U.S. Bureau of the Census, *Statistical Abstract of the United States: 1978* ((Washington: Government Printing Office 1978), pp. 356-361.

55. Bremner, *American Philanthropy,* p. 130.

56. For a thoughtful discussion of the considerations affecting relationships between professional fundraisers and lay persons, see John R. Seeley, *et al., Community Chest* (Toronto: University of Toronto Press, 1957).

Chapter 5
Post-Industrial America

1. Winfred Bell, *Aid to Dependent Children* (New York: Columbia University Press, 1965), p. 198.

2. Martha Derthick, *Policy Making for Social Security* (Washington: Brookings Institution, 1979), p. 340.

3. Bremner, *Philanthropy,* p. 145.

4. Ann Geddes, *Trends in Relief Expenditures,* 1910-1935 (New York: De Cappo Press, 1971), p. 96.

5. Geddes, *Relief,* p. 96.

6. For background on Townsend, and the pension and social security movement in general, see Abraham Holtzman, *The Townsend Movement* (New York: Brookman Associates, 1963).

7. See, e.g., Lubove, *Struggle,* p. 178.

8. See, e.g., Paul Samuelson, *Economics,* 10th Edition (New York: McGraw-Hill, 1976), p. 577-578.

9. The history and the current economic status of the Act are given in numerous works, including Robert M. Ball, *Social Security, Today and Tomorrow* (New York: Columbia University Press, 1978); Michael J. Baskin, ed., *The Crisis in Social Security* (San Francisco: Institute for Contemporary Studies, 1977); Rita Ricardo Campbell, *Social Security: Promise and Reality* (Stanford, Ca.: Hoover Institute, 1977); Martha Derthick, *Policy Making for Social Security* (Washington: Brookings Institution, 1977); John L. Palmer and Joseph J. Minarik, "Income Security Priorities," in *Setting National Priorities,* ed. Henry Owen and Charles L. Schultze (Washington: Brookings Institution, 1976), pp. 505-582; and A. Hayeworth Robertson, *Social Security: Prospects for Change* (Washington: William M. Mercer, 1978).

10. Munnell, *The Future of Social Security,* pp. 158 *et seq.*

11. U. S. Senate, Special Committee on Aging, 93rd Congress, 2nd Session, Future Directions in Social Security, Unresolved Issues: An Interim Staff Report, March, 1975 (Washington: Government Printing Office, 1975), p. 16.

12. For an early recognition of this phenomenon, see David Riesman, "Leisure in Post-Industrial Society," in *Abundance for What?* ed. Riesman (Garden City, New York: Doubleday, 1964), pp. 162-182; a more elaborate discussion is found in Daniel Bell, *The Coming of Post-Industrial Society* (New York: Basic Books, 1973).

13. All of the referenced data in the rest of this chapter are derived from the *Statistical Abstract, 1978.*

14. For some discussion of the modes of interaction typical in post-industrial suburbs, see Edward A. Wynne, *Growing Up Suburban* (Austin, Texas: University of Texas Press, 1977), especially Chapter 1.

15. See Philip Cusick, *Inside High School* (New York: Holt, Rinehart and Winston, 1973) and Edward A. Wynne, *Looking At Schools* (Lexington, Mass: Heath/Lexington, 1980).

16. Northeastern Illinois Suburban Planning Commission, *Suburban Factbook, 1973* (Chicago: Northeastern Planning Commission, 1973), pp. 31-33.

17. Neal E. Cutler and Robert A. Harootyan, "Demography of the Aged," in *Aging,* ed. James E. Birren and Diana S. Woodruff (New York: D. Van Nostrand, 1975), p. 57.

18. Palmer, "Income Security" p. 525.

19. See, e.g., Roy Bailey and Mike Brakes, eds., *Radical Social Work* (New York: Pantheon, 1977) and Richard A. Cloward and Frances Fox Pliven, *Regulating the Poor* (New York: Pantheon, 1971). For a sign of slight modification in this posture, see Willard Gaylin, *et al., Doing Good* (New York: Pantheon Books, 1978).

20. A newspaper story provides a typical example of this pursuit of triviality. The story is titled, "A Giant Baseball Bat Sculpture Dedicated in Chicago Ceremony," (Seth S. King, *New York Times,* April 15, 1977, p. 14). The $100,000 "sculpture" by Claes Oldenburg is a 101 foot structure, financed by federal funds, and representing a baseball bat. It was erected in front of the new offices of the Great Lakes Center for Social Security Administration. One bystander was quoted as follows: "I think it's ridiculous to spend $100,000 to put up a baseball bat in front of the Social Security building. Why didn't they buy a statue of some old people or something like that?" Unfortunately, the bystander's "simple" query would take a book to answer adequately.

21. For an inventory of some of our efforts to hide the reality of death from the living, see Kurt W. Back and Hans W. Baade, "The Social Meaning of Death and the Law," in *Aging and Social Policy,* ed. John McKinney and Frank T. de Vyver (New York: Appleton-Century-Crofts, 1966), pp. 302-330.

22. *Elrod v. Burns,* 427 U.S. 347 (1976). The Supreme Court held that it was a violation of free speech for the Illinois legislature to make half the clerical jobs in a county sheriff's office available for patronage purposes, i.e., jobholders were hired, *inter alia,* on the basis of their party loyalty, and if their "side" lost, they were replaced by the winner's supporters. The Court majority concluded that this practice unconstitutionally interfered with the rights of the jobholders to take political positions — and articulate them — without fear of retaliation. Or, one could say, the Court held there could be no direct personal consequences for persons having such opinions. But what is this world where our opinions and words may not have

direct consequences?

23. *Shapiro v. Thompson,* 394 U. S. 618, 89 S. Ct. 1322 (1968. A majority of the Supreme Court held that it was an unconstitutional intrusion on the equal right of all citizens to travel for a state to condition eligibility for state welfare aid on an applicant's having resided in the state for at least a year. Among the arguments offered by states in support of the residency requirement was the proposition that without such residence, it would be difficult to acquire enough information about the applicant to know if the applicant was "deserving," i.e., to insure that the information submitted by the applicant was truthful. The majority observed that this problem would be comparatively easily handled by the state's corresponding with the welfare office in the applicant's original home area. The Court's proposal is a classic example of the awkwardness of formal enforcement of reciprocity; the "policing" capabilities of one's neighbors, employers, and relatives are obviously far more powerful than information collected from corresponding with a remote agency.

24. For general discussion of these trends, see Sanford J. Fox, "Child's Legal Responsibility for Support of Parents," *Journal of Geriatric Psychiatry* 5, no. 2 (1972): 137-147 and Alvin L. Shorr, *Filial Responsibility in the Modern American Family* (Washington: Government Printing Office, 1960), U. S. Department of Health, Education and Welfare, Social Security Administration. Some sense of the tone of these writings can be attained when we realize that Fox observed that he was against encouraging policies "rooted in Elizabethan England" — as if the longevity of a policy was, *per se,* a sign of inappropriateness. That perspective would abolish the Ten Commandments!

25. The egalitarian position is represented by Christopher Jencks *et al., Inequality* (New York: Basic Books, 1972) and John Rawles, *A Theory of Justice* (Cambridge, Mass.: Harvard University Press, 1971). For the opposite position, see Robert Nisbet, "The Pursuit of Equality," *The Public Interest,* no. 35 (Spring, 1974): 103-120.

26. Riley, Riley, and Johnson, *Aging and Society,* vol. 1, p. 105.

27. See, e.g., Palmer and Minarik, "Income Security," and Michael C. Barth, George J. Carcagno, and John L. Palmer, *Toward an*

Effective Income Support System (Madison, Wisconsin: Institute for Research on Poverty, 1974).

28. Milton Friedman, "Can Freedom Prevail?" *Newsweek* 94, no. 21 (November 19, 1979), p. 142.

29. Robert A. Moffitt and Kenneth C. Keher, "The Effect of Tax and Transfer Programs on Labor Supply," in *Research in Labor Economics,* ed. Ronald Ehrenberg (Greenwich, Conn.: J A I Press, forthcoming).

30. John Bishop, "The Welfare Brief," *The Public Interest,* no. 53 (Fall 1978), 175. Another commentator was more critical of this fear of dependency. He observed that "In American society...'dependent character' is a highly derogatory term, and a person so described is thought to be in need of psychological help." Margaret Clar, "Cultural Values and Dependency in Later Life," in *Aging and Modernization,* ed. Cowgill and Holmes, p. 271. For a similarly critical analysis, see Doi, *Dependence.*

31. Consider the following typical statement by a proponent of increased welfare benefits: "For example, by 1961, German payroll taxes for social insurance had reached 22.3 percent, counting both employer and employee contributions. A common theme in German public discourse was that people would not tolerate further increases. By 1973, payroll taxes covering pensions and compulsory health insurance had climbed to more than 27 percent — with hardly any political fuss. Compare our present [United States] 11.7 of taxable pay, which includes employer and employee contributions and a special levy for Medicare." Harold L. Wilensky, "The Welfare Mess," *Society 13,* no. 4 (May/June, 1976): 13.

32. Edward Cowan, "Social Security Commissioner Calls Improvements Unlikely," *New York Times,* July 12, 1979, p. A10.

33. Milton L. Rakove, *We Don't Want Nobody Nobody Sent* (Bloomington, Ind.: University of Indiana Press, 1979) p. 318.

34. Riley, Riley, and Johnson, *Aging and Society,* vol. 1, p. 542.

35. Riley, Riley, and Johnson, *Aging and Society,* vol. 1, p. 552.

36. For similar conclusions, see Irving Rosow, *Social Integration of the Aged* (New York: The Free Press, 1967) and Rosow, *Socialization to Old Age* (Berkeley, California: University of California Press, 1974). Much of this research is summarized in Judith Treas, "Aging and the Family," in *Aging,* ed. Birren and Woodruff, pp. 95-97.

37. See Bernice L. Neugarten, "Age Groups in America and the Rise of the Young-Old," *Annals of the American Academy* (September, 1974): 187-198.

38. Marvin B. Sussman, "The Urban Kin Networks in the Formulation of Family Theory," in *Families in East and West,* ed. Ruben Hill and Rene Konig (The Hague: Mouton, 1970), pp. 481-503.

39. See Arlie R. Hochschild, *The Unexpected Community* (Englewood Cliffs, New Jersey: Prentice-Hall, 1967); Rosow, *Integration;* and Bernice L. Neugarten and Gunhild O. Hagestad, "Age Status and the Life Course," in *Handbook of Aging and the Social Sciences,"* ed. James E. Birren and Ethyl Shanas (New York: Van Nostrand Rinehold, 1976).

40. Rosow, *Integration.*

41. Erdman Palmore, *The Honorable Elders* (Durham, North Carolina: Duke University Press, 1975).

42. See Riley, Riley, and Johnson, *Aging and Society,* vol. 1, p. 257, and K. Warner Schaie, "Age Changes in Adult Intelligence," *Aging,* ed. Birren and Woodruff, pp. 111-124.

43. Riley, Riley, and Johnson, *Aging and Society,* vol. 1, p. 473.

44. R. H. Binstock, "Aging and the Future of American Politics," *The Anals* 415 (1974): 199-212.

45. Richard E. Barfield and James N. Morgan, *Early Retirement* (Ann Arbor, Michigan: Institute for Social Research, 1974).

46. Erwin Palmore, "Why Do People Retire?" *Aging and Human Development* 2, no. 4 (November 1971): 271.

47. Vern L. Bengston and David A. Haber, "Sociological Approaches to Aging," in *Aging,* ed. Birren and Woodruff, pp. 83 ff.

48. See Zena Smith Blau, *Old Age in a Changing Society* (New York: Franklin Watts, 1974), pp. 135, ff., for a discussion of the forms of pressure applied by younger co-workers to encourage early retirement.

49. The data from this study were made available to me on a confidential basis — perhaps because their implications were embarrassing to the company's personnel policies, which emphasized formal education requirements.

50. See, e.g., Samuelson, *Economics,* pp. 577-78.

Chapter 6
Forecasting, Analyzing and Prescribing

1. W. J. Bate, ed. *The Selected Writings of Edmund Burke* (New York: Modern Library, 1960), pp. 248-249.

2. Unless otherwise noted, all data cited in this chapter are from the *Statistical Abstract, 1978.*

3. Cutler and Harootyan, "Demography."

4. The nations involved were Canada, France, Italy, Japan, Germany, and the United Kingdom.

5. For a recent criticism of our over-valuation of formal education, see Richard Freeman, *The Over Educated America* (New York: Academic Press, 1976).

6. For discussion on the characteristics of post-industrial suburbs, see Edward A. Wynne, *Growing Up Suburban* (Austin, Texas: University of Texas Press, 1977).

7. Essentially, the criticism in the text is directed at the modern, bureaucratic, comparatively large, departmentalized, cognitively-focused school (or college) with low levels of pupil/pupil and pupil/teacher emotional interaction. Such forms of education are tending to pervade industrial countries and post-industrial countries. However, different educational patterns have existed in the past, and, to a lesser degree, still are followed in some industrial environments today. For examples of both earlier and contemporary forms of variation, see Roger G. Barker and Paul V. Gump, *Big School, Small School* (Stanford, CA.:

Stanford University Press, 1964); Urie Bronfenbrenner, *Two Worlds of Childhood* (New York: Russel Sage, 1970); Yehudi A. Cohen, "Schools and Civilizational States," in *The Social Sciences and the Comparative Study of Education Systems,* ed. Joseph Fischer (Scranton, Pa.: International Textbook Co., 1970), pp. 55-147; Edward D. Meyers, *Education in the Perspective of History* (New York: Holt, Rinehart and Winston, 1964); George Richmond, *The Micro-Society School* (New York: Harper and Row, 1973); and Wynne, *Looking at Schools.* See also some of the references on the "voucher system," in Note 13, below.

8. As an instance of this disregard of the role of education as a transmittor of good character, consider the following anecdote. The Council for Basic Education is a respected national organization dedicated to increasing cognitive learning among school children. It was formed as a partial reaction to many of the "softer" elements of progressive education. Among educators, its policies are usually viewed as conservative. In an interview the Council's associate director made the following statement: "Education is for the intellectual development of the individual. Education is not for the purpose of the state...we think that well-education people will be better citizens because they are well educated and it's their education that then makes them better citizens....We are for a sound education which we regard in terms of individual development, not special purpose....a well-educated person is going to be a better citizen insofar as he chooses to take part in citizenship affairs." *Looking At,* November 1976, ERIC Clearinghouse on Social Studies/Social Sciences Education, Boulder, Co., p. 3. Obviously, the Council's associate director does not believe in the *duty* of active citizenship, nor (implicitly) in the duty to help others. Their view of virtue is essentially passive — don't do wrong.

10. Peter F. Drucker, "What We Can Learn From Japanese Management," in *Men, Ideas and Politics,* ed. Drucker (New York: Harper and Row, 1971).

11. For a modern example of youth learning from their elders, see Eliot Wigginton, ed., *The Foxfire Book* (Garden City, New York: Doubleday, 1972).

12. Palmer, *Elders.*

13. For instance, in the late 1960's, it was proposed that a new system of citizen/school relations — called the voucher system — be tried (and a federal subsidy was offered to any school district that would try it). Only one of the 23,000 American school districts was willing to try the system. It is unlikely that all the other 22,999 districts seriously doubted the merits of the basic idea. It is more likely that the obstacles arose from (a) the inhibitions the government attached to its offer to satisfy various interest groups, (b) national pressures from hostile teacher groups, (c) the resistance of other national interest groups. In other words, without these various national interest groups (including the federal grovernment), it is certainly possible that some districts in America might have read of the idea, gone ahead, and tried it. The operation of the voucher system actually did not involve spending more money. But a limited experiment in one small school district became practically a Verdun. For some background on voucher developments, see, e.g., Stephen Arons, "Equity, Options and Vouchers," *Teachers College Record* 72, no. 3 (February 1971): 325-340, and Irene Solet, "Education Vouchers: An Inquiry and Analysis," *Journal of Law and Education* 1, no. 2 (April 1972): 315-330.

Appendix

1. For references on the data presented, see Edward A. Wynne, "Behind the Discipline Problem: Youth Suicide as a Measure of Alienation," *Phi Delta Kappan* 59 (January 1978): 307-315, and Wynne, "Facts About the Character of Young Americans," *Character,* 1 *no. 1* (November, 1979): 1-8.

INDEX

Adults as socializers, 25. *See also* Aged

Affluence affecting socialization, 135, increase in, 135

Age groups: assistance among, 3 et seq., defined, 30. *See also* Cohorts; Generations

Aged: changing retirement patterns, 118, 152; compared to younger persons, 157 et seq., comparatively powerless, 31; counterdonations by, 56; creation of social security, and, 130; economic status of, 146; Great Depression, in, 108 et seq.; industrial revolution, in, 108 et seq.; postponing retirement, 185; pre-industrial societies, in, 56 et seq.; role in Japan, 156; teachers, as, 181; values and conduct of, 151 et seq.; volunteers, as, 178; without retirement, 56

Aid to families of dependent children, 123

Alcoholics, 20

Altruism analyzed, 45

Architecture and reciprocity 25

Aristotle, 50

Authority: over children, 15 et seq.; parents and, 15 et seq.

Becket, Thomas, 69

Beggars identified by deformities, 49, and provisions of the Poor Law, 90

Bentham, Jeremy, 1

Carnegie, Andrew, 112

Catholic Church: as mediating agency, 23; holidays and, 44; St. Paul and, 105

Ceremonies: birth, at, 24; Catholic Church and, 44; communicating cohort responsibilities, 55; fame and, 71; Nazi Germany and, 44; reciprocity and, 24, 39; recom-mendations about, 186; socialization and, 43; wedding as, 44

Chalmers, Thomas, 99 et seq., psychology of, 102; themes criticized by, 127, 176

Charity contrasted with reciprocity, 104, informal enforcement of, 111, principal distorted, 145

Charity Organization Societies, 116 et seq.

Children: counterdonations by, 15 et seq.; donations to, 15 et seq., 32 et seq.; learning reciprocity, 14 et seq.; as producers, 56

Christianity and reciprocity, 51 et seq.

Churches as mediating agencies, 25

Cicero, 50

Clients, 50

Cohorts: changes in relations among, 135, 139 et seq.; costs of dependent, 168 et seq.; defined, 31; diminishing segregation, 185; intercohort relations in Europe, 150; responsibilities of, 55; segregation in schools, 137; *See also* Age groups, Generations

Colleges. *See* Schools

Compact, 4

Contract and formal enforcement, 49 et seq.

Counterdonation, 10, by aged, 56, compared to pure dependency, 164, dead, to, 66 et seq., fame as, 70, made apparent to children, 25, symbolic, 30

Courts and student rights, 142, law of settlement and, 144

Dead: counterdonations to, 66 et seq.; donations by, 2, 4, 66 et seq.; fame and, 71; forgetting, 74; mediating institutions and, 74

WESTMAR COLLEGE LIBRARY